# THE PRESIDENT'S NEW CUBA POLICY AND U.S. NATIONAL SECURITY

## HEARING

BEFORE THE

### SUBCOMMITTEE ON
### THE WESTERN HEMISPHERE

OF THE

## COMMITTEE ON FOREIGN AFFAIRS
## HOUSE OF REPRESENTATIVES

ONE HUNDRED FOURTEENTH CONGRESS

FIRST SESSION

FEBRUARY 26, 2015

**Serial No. 114–26**

Printed for the use of the Committee on Foreign Affairs

Available via the World Wide Web: http://www.foreignaffairs.house.gov/ or
http://www.gpo.gov/fdsys/

U.S. GOVERNMENT PUBLISHING OFFICE

93–534PDF                    WASHINGTON : 2015

For sale by the Superintendent of Documents, U.S. Government Publishing Office
Internet: bookstore.gpo.gov   Phone: toll free (866) 512–1800; DC area (202) 512–1800
Fax: (202) 512–2104   Mail: Stop IDCC, Washington, DC 20402–0001

## COMMITTEE ON FOREIGN AFFAIRS

EDWARD R. ROYCE, California, *Chairman*

| | |
|---|---|
| CHRISTOPHER H. SMITH, New Jersey | ELIOT L. ENGEL, New York |
| ILEANA ROS-LEHTINEN, Florida | BRAD SHERMAN, California |
| DANA ROHRABACHER, California | GREGORY W. MEEKS, New York |
| STEVE CHABOT, Ohio | ALBIO SIRES, New Jersey |
| JOE WILSON, South Carolina | GERALD E. CONNOLLY, Virginia |
| MICHAEL T. McCAUL, Texas | THEODORE E. DEUTCH, Florida |
| TED POE, Texas | BRIAN HIGGINS, New York |
| MATT SALMON, Arizona | KAREN BASS, California |
| DARRELL E. ISSA, California | WILLIAM KEATING, Massachusetts |
| TOM MARINO, Pennsylvania | DAVID CICILLINE, Rhode Island |
| JEFF DUNCAN, South Carolina | ALAN GRAYSON, Florida |
| MO BROOKS, Alabama | AMI BERA, California |
| PAUL COOK, California | ALAN S. LOWENTHAL, California |
| RANDY K. WEBER SR., Texas | GRACE MENG, New York |
| SCOTT PERRY, Pennsylvania | LOIS FRANKEL, Florida |
| RON DeSANTIS, Florida | TULSI GABBARD, Hawaii |
| MARK MEADOWS, North Carolina | JOAQUIN CASTRO, Texas |
| TED S. YOHO, Florida | ROBIN L. KELLY, Illinois |
| CURT CLAWSON, Florida | BRENDAN F. BOYLE, Pennsylvania |
| SCOTT DesJARLAIS, Tennessee | |
| REID J. RIBBLE, Wisconsin | |
| DAVID A. TROTT, Michigan | |
| LEE M. ZELDIN, New York | |
| TOM EMMER, Minnesota | |

AMY PORTER, *Chief of Staff*     THOMAS SHEEHY, *Staff Director*

JASON STEINBAUM, *Democratic Staff Director*

————

## SUBCOMMITTEE ON THE WESTERN HEMISPHERE

JEFF DUNCAN, South Carolina, *Chairman*

| | |
|---|---|
| CHRISTOPHER H. SMITH, New Jersey | ALBIO SIRES, New Jersey |
| ILEANA ROS-LEHTINEN, Florida | JOAQUIN CASTRO, Texas |
| MICHAEL T. McCAUL, Texas | ROBIN L. KELLY, Illinois |
| MATT SALMON, Arizona | GREGORY W. MEEKS, New York |
| RON DeSANTIS, Florida | ALAN GRAYSON, Florida |
| TED S. YOHO, Florida | ALAN S. LOWENTHAL, California |
| TOM EMMER, Minnesota | |

(II)

# CONTENTS

# THE PRESIDENT'S NEW CUBA POLICY AND U.S. NATIONAL SECURITY

---

### THURSDAY, FEBRUARY 26, 2015

House of Representatives,
Subcommittee on the Western Hemisphere,
Committee on Foreign Affairs,
*Washington, DC.*

The subcommittee met, pursuant to notice, at 10 o'clock a.m., in room 2167 Rayburn House Office Building, Hon. Jeff Duncan (chairman of the subcommittee) presiding.

Mr. DUNCAN. Okay. A quorum being present, the subcommittee will come to order.

I will start by recognizing myself and then the ranking member to present our opening statements, and then we will recognize the witnesses as well. So we will go ahead and get started.

In July 1985, President Ronald Reagan outlined Cuba's support for terrorism since the 1960s through its actions in openly arming, training, and directing terrorists operating on at least three continents, in Latin America, Africa, and the Middle East. Reagan also cited repeated sanctions by the Organization of American States against Castro for sponsoring terrorism in places and countries too numerous to mention.

During this time, Cuba was also hosting a Soviet combat brigade, a submarine base capable of servicing Soviet submarines, and a military base that Soviet military aircraft regularly used. Cuba's actions landed it on the State Sponsors of Terrorism list in 1982, and it has remained there ever since. President Obama's announcement in December 2014 that the U.S. would reconsider the terrorism designation as a part of its pursuit of normalized relations with Cuba is deeply concerning given Cuba's record on multiple levels.

I would like to enter into the record at this point an article that says—it is, "Cuba Says Fast Track to Restoring Ties Depends on the U.S.," and in the article it says that the U.S. needs to remove them from the State Sponsors of Terrorism list if we are to move forward. So I will enter that in the record. Without objection, so ordered.

Today I want to consider the U.S. national security implications of President Obama's Cuba policy shift and potential vulnerabilities to America as a result. First, Cuba's record of supporting terrorism and violence in the Western Hemisphere threatens the U.S. national security interest in the region.

(1)

According to the State Department's country reports on terrorism in 2013, which was issued in April 2014, Cuba has long provided safe haven to members of the Basque Fatherland and Liberty, or ETA, and the Revolutionary Armed Forces of Colombia, known as FARC, both considered foreign terrorist organizations by the United States. Cuba also continues to harbor fugitives wanted in the United States through providing support, such as housing, food ration, books, and medical care.

Furthermore, the U.S. fugitives, such as Joanne Chesimard—and I don't know if I pronounced that correctly—who is on the FBI's Most Wanted Terrorism list, remain protected by the Cuban Government for their crimes against the Americas.

In addition, according to the Institute for Cuban and Cuban American Studies at the University of Miami, Cuba provides intelligence to Hezbollah and Hamas. For instance, Arab Shiites Ghazi Nasr Al Dan and Fawzi Kanaan based in Venezuela coordinate with the Cuban Government to raise funds for Hezbollah and facilitate Hezbollah's travel in the region. Likewise, Hezbollah and Cuba, a Hamas-funded Turkish charity, operates in Havana and is a member of the Union of Good, an entity that financially supports Hamas.

Second, Cuba's record as a foreign intelligence collector and trafficker threatens United States national security and the safety of Americans. Overt in its espionage against the United States, and in selling U.S. national security secrets to other regimes, such as Venezuela and Iran, Cuban intelligence services have been described by former CIA Cuban Analyst Brian Latell as among the four or five best anywhere in the world.

In 2002, Defense Intelligence Agency Analyst Ana Montes was convicted of spying for Cuban intelligence for 16 years. This month, the DIA Director, Lieutenant General Vincent Stewart, maintained that foreign intelligence threats from Russia, China, and Cuban intelligence services continue to be a challenge with Cuban intelligence services remaining the predominant counterintelligence threat to the United States emanating from Latin America.

American tourists or businessmen and women who visit Cuba could find themselves subjected to Cuban surveillance. By staying in hotels, which are run by the way by the Cuban military and staffed by Cuban intelligence agents wired for video and audio recording, American visitors are prey for Cuban espionage.

In view of this, I believe it is critical that the Obama administration fully assess these potentially great vulnerabilities to American citizens and its review of Cuba's sponsorship of terrorism. Any attempt by the Obama administration to delist Cuba without first providing Congress with a comprehensive damage assessment of Cuba's counterintelligence activities against Americans could invite even more Cuban espionage against unsuspecting Americans in the future.

Thirdly, Cuba's relationship with hostile regimes, such as Iran, North Korea, Russia, Syria, and Venezuela, threaten U.S. national security interests. Cuba is a strong supporter of Iran's illicit nuclear program and the Assad regime's brutality against its people in Syria. In July 2013, Cuba was caught red-handed proliferating illicit military equipment, including fighter jobs, surface-to-air missile system components, and ammunition to North Korea, illegally circumventing the U.N. embargo.

In Venezuela, Cuba has trained pro-Maduro groups who use violence against Venezuelan student protesters, and media reports in January of this year found that hundreds of Cuban military personnel had been stationed in Venezuela. Most significant for the U.S. homeland, Cuban-Russian relations have continued to deepen.

In February of last year, 2014, the Russian Defense Minister stated that Russia wants to build a military base in several countries in our hemisphere, including Cuba. In April 2014, the U.S. observed two Russian ships operating in waters beyond the U.S. territorial seas near Cuba, and press reports suggested that the ships were part of a spying operation against the U.S.

Furthermore, in July of last year, Russian President Vladimir Putin visited Cuba and forgave 90 percent of Cuba's debt since the Soviet period—the largest debt forgiveness agreement in Russian history. Now, what is that all about?

Press reports have also stated that Russia and Cuba agreed to reopen the Lourdes base, an electronic listening post, which is only 150 miles from the United States coast. Last month, a Russian signals intelligence ship made an unannounced visit to Cuba on the eve of U.S. talks with Cuba in Havana on restoring diplomatic relations. And also, last month, Cuban President Raul Castro demanded that the U.S. hand back the U.S. naval station in Guantanamo Bay, Cuba, before Cuba and the U.S. could attain normalized relations.

Given Cuba's alliances with unsavory regimes, the U.S. national security impact of complying with such brash demands would sever the U.S. military efforts in the region. Gitmo is the oldest overseas U.S. naval base and only permanent DoD base in the region. It is critical for U.S. national security interests, and it houses not only the Joint Task Force Guantanamo, but also the Homeland Security and State Department's Migrant Operations Center. Its location enables U.S. forces to maintain strategic operational and tactical advantages across a full spectrum of military operations and regional security cooperation efforts.

Fourth, a criminal pipeline from Cuba to Florida threatens the United States' national security interest with Cuban migrants exploiting U.S. law, stealing from the American taxpayer, and paying the Cuban Government to live large off the cash in Cuba.

In January 2015, South Florida's Sun Sentinel published the findings of a year-long investigation which showed that crooks from Cuba had robbed American businesses and taxpayers of more than $2 billion over two decades. Cuba benefits from organized crime rings operating in Cuba and the United States.

For example, in Miami-Dade County, Florida, where 24 percent of the population was born in Cuba, immigrants from the island account for 73 percent of arrests for health care fraud, 72 percent of arrests for cargo theft, 59 percent of arrests for marijuana trafficking, and half of the arrests for credit card and insurance fraud.

However, Cuba exploitation of Americans is not limited just to Florida. According to the Sun Sentinel's analysis, over the past two decades Cuba natives with addresses in Florida have been convicted in 34 states, Puerto Rico, and Washington, DC. In addition, a 2012 case showed that a Cuban crime ring stole 22,000 credit card numbers and then used them to buy 60,000 gift cards worth $15 million from Walmart stores in 45 states and Puerto Rico.

Some of the convicted individuals learned their illicit trade in Cuba before immigrating to the United States, and some fugitives who returned to Cuba had to give the government a cut of the money benefitting the Castro regime. The investigation also found that the Obama administration's recent Cuba policy change in loosening U.S. regulation on travel and money to Cuba may actually increase organized crime as well.

This is particularly concerning given the surge in Cuban migration in the United States following the Cuba policy change. According to the U.S. Coast Guard, Cuban migrant flow increased 68 percent from 2013 to 2014, and Cuban migration to the U.S. is also much higher thus far in 2015 than it was at the same time last year.

In conclusion, Cuba's role in supporting terrorism and violence, conducting foreign intelligence operations against the United States, partnering with global bad actors, and enabling a criminal pipeline from Cuba to Florida is clear. Such a record necessitates that we carefully examine the impact that the Obama administration's Cuban policy change may have on U.S. national security and Cuba's ability to more easily conduct its illicit operations. Today's hearing could not be more timely given that U.S. and Cuban officials meet in Washington tomorrow to continue discussing reestablishment of diplomatic relations.

With that, I will turn to the ranking member, Mr. Sires, for his opening statement. I look forward to a very robust hearing today, providing information to Members of Congress, as we move forward addressing these policy changes.

So, Mr. Sires is recognized for an opening statement.

Mr. SIRES. First, let me thank you, Chairman, for holding this hearing, and thank all the people that are here today.

It has been no secret that I have been disappointed and concerned regarding the administration plans to loosening sanctions, initiating discussion to reestablish diplomatic relationships with the Cuban regime. I understand talks have just started, but preliminary and secret negotiations were taking place for months prior to the President's announcement this past December. Neither prior nor since the December announcement has the Cuban regime relented its practice of restraining the Cuban people and abusing their human rights.

Just days after the December announcement, Raul Castro dispelled any misgiving and declared that the regime would not abandon its Communist path, let alone lose any stronghold over the Cuban people. And what should have been a joyous moment to celebrate the release of Alan Gross was clouded by the actions taken by the administration to secure his release.

I also find that easing of travel and commercial restriction was misguided, as it will only boost revenues for enabling state-controlled economy, and the administration has clearly fell short in failing to secure the return of fugitives. Joanne Chesimard, the FBI's number one Most Wanted Terrorist, has remained free in

Cuba for 30 years after having murdered New Jersey State Trooper Warner Foerster and escaping to Cuba.

What is astonishing is that all of—for all the talks of additional actions to be taken by the United States, little has been said of the steps that the Cuban regime must take. In my opinion, far too much has been given already. We need to see more concrete measures in terms of human rights, political freedoms, and the release of all political prisoners permanently, and that is just the beginning.

And yet for their part Cuban authorities have not only made clear that futures such as Chesimard's are off the table, but that relations cannot be normalized unless the U.S. lifts the embargo, returns Guantanamo, and abandons support of Cuba's dissidents that do nothing more than advocate for freedom and respect for human rights. If that were not enough, Cuban authorities are also insisting on being removed from the State Department's State Sponsors of Terrorists list.

This is a dangerous and concerning action that I feel the administration has prematurely conceded to consider. I feel that before any consideration is given to removing Cuba from the State Sponsors of Terrorists list that Cuba should, for its part, return the FBI number one terrorist, Joanne Chesimard, alongside the countless U.S. fugitives hiding in Cuba.

The Cuban regime claims its innocence in regards to its designation on the state-sponsored terrorism list, but the Cuban regime's actions have been anything but innocent. The Cuban regime has a long and sordid history of supporting anti-U.S. intelligence efforts and colluding with questionable state actors like Russia, North Korea, and Venezuela, whose governments espouse anti-Americanism and pose a security concern to either their neighbors or their own people.

The U.S. Defense Intelligence Agency has—was penetrated by Cuban spy Ana Montes, undetected for an astonishing 16 years until detained in 2001. Most recently, in 2013, Panamanian authorities seized a North Korean freighter declared to be carrying 10,000 tons of sugar from Cuba only to discover a hidden cargo of Soviet-made anti-missile system components, fighter jet parts, and engines. And in July 2014, a United Nations panel of experts determined that both the shipment and the transactions between Cuba and North Korea were in violation of the U.N. sanctions.

Trust must be earned. It is not just given. The Cuban regime forfeited that privilege over 50 years ago and has done nothing since to garner the trust of the Cuban people or the international community. While I do not agree with the direction our administration has taken in regards to Cuba, I implore the United States to proceed with caution and not to concede to any of the Cuban's regime's demands until more significant steps are taken.

Thank you.

Mr. DUNCAN. I thank the ranking member. The Chair will now recognize one of my heroes in Congress and the former chairwoman of the full committee, Ms. Ros-Lehtinen from Florida, for her opening statement for as long as she wants to——

Ms. ROS-LEHTINEN. Thank you so much, Mr. Chairman. Thank you for your dedication to freedom and democracy and for calling this important and timely hearing. Let me be clear: Cuba poses a clear and present danger to the United States. The Castro regime undermines our national security at every turn and reinforces instability in the entire region by exporting the Cuban military and espionage apparatus across the region.

The ALBA countries have secret security advisors who are Cuban nationals. Some ALBA countries even send diplomats overseas who are undercover Cuban agents. Cuba is an avowed enemy of the United States, and let me cite these bullet points just in the recent years that the Castro regime has done. Has killed American citizens in the Brothers to the Rescue shootdown 19 years ago this week. Has worked with the Russians to try to reopen the Lourdes spy facility in Cuba. Has allowed Russian spy ships to dock in Havana as recently as just a few days ago. Was caught sending arms and military equipment last year to North Korea in violation of multiple U.N. Security Council resolutions.

The Castro regime is hiding U.S. fugitives of law and has given asylum to Joanne Chesimard, who is considered a Most Wanted Terrorist by our FBI. It has given safe haven to terrorist groups such as the FARC and ETA, has sent military advisors to Venezuela who have caused the deaths of many Venezuelans due to the violence perpetrated by the thugs of Nicolas Maduro.

The Castro regime has penetrated our own intelligence services with spies working for the Castro regime, like Ana Belen Montes and Kendall Myers, had Cuban agents torture and beat American POWs at a prison camp in North Vietnam known as the Zoo, has sent troops to Angola in 1970s and '80s to further destabilize the country and fight alongside leftist movements contrary to U.S. security interests, has ties with Iran, with Russia, with Syria, and the list goes on, Mr. Chairman, yet all of these realities have been ignored by the Obama administration.

Tomorrow, as we have pointed out, the Department of State will roll out the red carpet for officials from the Castro regime. The lead negotiator for the Castro regime is Josefina Vidal, who was a Cuban spy in the United States who was actually kicked out, along with her husband, from the U.S. due to their illicit espionage activities. And now she is negotiating for the Castro regime.

I firmly believe that the President's concessions to the Castro brothers on December 17 pose a real national security threat, and here's why. It is well-known that Cuba has one of the world's most advanced espionage apparatus, and that apparatus is aimed right at our country and here, very much active in our nation's capital in Washington, DC.

We know that Cuba has had spies on the Hill and in many U.S. Government agencies, so the President's new policies will provide an injection of new money to the regime, millions of dollars, and this new money will go straight into the pockets of the Castro brothers and the Cuban military, which owns and operates the tourist industry in Cuba.

With this new infusion of capital, the Cubans will be able to provide more resources toward their espionage activities directed at us. And what will they do with the intelligence that they gather? They will sell it to our enemies, to the highest bidder on the black market. These are just some of the reasons, Mr. Chairman, of why

Cuba does pose a national security threat to the U.S., and why it should remain on the State Sponsors of Terrorism list. The White House must stop putting politics ahead of our national security.

On July 3, 1961, President Eisenhower terminated diplomatic relations with Cuba after the Cuban regime decided to expel several United States personnel from Havana. President Eisenhower responded by stating, and I quote, ''This calculated action on the part of the Castro Government is only the latest of a long series of harassments, baseless accusations, and vilification.'' Eisenhower continued, ''There is a limit to what the United States and self-respect can endure. That limit has now been reached. Meanwhile, our sympathy goes out to the people of Cuba now suffering under the yoke of a dictator.''

President Obama should learn from history that negotiating with the Castro regime is a failed endeavor.

And with that, Mr. Chairman, I would ask unanimous consent to enter into the record a letter addressed to President Obama signed by the mayors of the city of Miami, Coral Gables, and Doral expressing their opposition to the December 17 accord.

Mr. DUNCAN. Without objection.

Ms. ROS-LEHTINEN. Thank you, Mr. Chairman.

Mr. DUNCAN. I want to thank the lady for her comments, and I will now—if any other member has an opening statement, just in the essence of time we will—okay. I am going to recognize the rest of the members for a minute, real quickly.

Mr. MEEKS. Thank you, Mr. Chair. Needless to say, I support the President's position and the President's opening diplomatic relations with Iran. What we need to look at, since 1960, 1959, have the policies that existed for over 50 years, has it been successful? Who agrees with us? Which countries? We have got allies all over. Has it helped us as members of the United States, or has it hurt us? Has it really changed the conditions for the people in Cuba?

And we know that there is a lot of work to be done. I am not saying that. We know that with diplomatic engagement there is a lot of hard work to be done.

But I challenge principally the Western Hemisphere. Canada doesn't agree with us; they are a strong ally. Colombia doesn't agree with us. Brazil doesn't agree with us. Chile doesn't agree with us. Peru doesn't agree with us. In fact, they say that that is the one thing the United States standing by itself has been a hindrance to working with everyone on the Western Hemisphere. We need to work collectively together, and in that way we can have the change that we are looking for.

I said yesterday it is difficult when you are trying to work in multilateral ways. Doing it unilaterally doesn't work. So I am saying let us focus to get the change that we need in Cuba, but let us get a policy that works because the policy that has been in existence for the last over 50 years has not been successful.

Mr. DUNCAN. The Chair will now recognize Mr. DeSantis from Florida for an opening statement.

Mr. DESANTIS. Thanks, Mr. Chairman. I don't think 1959 is as relevant as right now. Does this change benefit the Castro regime or the Cuban people fighting for freedom, or the American people?

I think the answer clearly is this is a lifeline for the Castro regime. They may be removed now off the State Sponsors of Terrorists list.

This is a regime, as my colleague from New Jersey said, Joanne Chesimard, she is being harbored there. She is on the FBI's top 10 Most Wanted Terrorists list. The Cuban Air Force officers who have been indicted by the Federal Grand Jury, they get medals in Cuba. They are not held to account. They have been caught shipping weapons, this regime, to North Korea, one of the worst regimes in the entire world.

And of course the Cuban military and the Cuban regime are working with Maduro's henchmen who are repressing the freedom fighters in Venezuela. And of course they have offered an operational presence in Cuba to Vladimir Putin's Russia. We have seen that, obviously, before in the past. So what exactly have they done to cause the U.S. to remove it from the State Sponsors of Terrorism? Nothing.

My friend on the other side of the aisle says we need to work multilaterally. These are unilateral concessions that this regime has done absolutely nothing to earn.

And I yield back.

Mr. DUNCAN. I am sure we will get into some of those topics, so let us go ahead and introduce our witnesses. Before I do, we are operating on a lighting system that you have in front of you. When I recognize you, it will turn green; you will have 5 minutes. When there is 1 minute remaining, it will turn yellow. That is a warning. And when it turns red, your time is up. Please finish your statement, finish your sentence, and then we will move on. We are going to try to stay on time with four witnesses.

So without further ado, I will recognize the witnesses. Mr. Simmons, for the panelists and for the committee, their bios are in our file, and they are made of record. I am not going to—I am going to dispense with reading their bios today in the essence of time.

So, Mr. Simmons, you are recognized for 5 minutes.

## STATEMENT OF MR. CHRIS SIMMONS, EDITOR, CUBA CONFIDENTIAL

Mr. SIMMONS. Mr. Chairman, thank you for the opportunity to testify on the national security threat posed by Cuba. As Washington considers a radical change in our relationship with Havana, Cuba's world-class espionage operations against us demand careful review and deliberation.

I had the privilege of serving as a counterintelligence officer with the U.S. Army and Defense Intelligence Agency for over 20 years. With regard to Cuba, I was deeply involved with most U.S. counterintelligence successes against Havana from 1996 through 2004. I was a central figure in the Ana Montes spy case, and the lead military official in the 2003 expulsion of 14 Cuban diplomat-spies.

Underestimated and misunderstood for more than half a century, Havana remains a clear and present danger to the United States. It is a national security state, and its miliary and intelligence agencies exist solely to ensure regime continuity. Its spy services are augmented by a million-member neighborhood informant program known as Committees for the Defense of the Revolution. These entities combine to give the regime an omnipresent intelligence structure that is, on a per capital basis, 34 times larger than that of the entire U.S. intelligence community.

Castro's spies also benefit from a narrow focus on just two enemies—the Cuban people and the United States. In fact, the regime has three separate intelligence agencies arrayed against the United States. One of these services, the vaunted Directorate of Intelligence, is now ranked fifth or sixth in the world.

Greed, not self-defense, is Cuba's sole motive for its espionage efforts against the United States. Havana long ago earned the nickname ''Intelligence Trafficker to the World,'' for its sale and barter of stolen U.S. secrets. Following the breakup of the Soviet Union and the loss of Moscow's $3 billion annual subsidy, its auctioning of U.S. classified information skyrocketed. Its information brokering is now a key source of revenue, earning hundreds of millions of dollars annually in goods, services, and cash.

The administration's current outreach offers five seemingly unanticipated consequences, which Havana will exploit as catalysts to increase espionage against the United States.

First, opening Cuba to U.S. travelers will bring a huge influx of desperately needed cash to Cuba's intelligence and security services that, along with their military brethren, run the entire tourism sector as profit-making enterprises.

Second, this flood of American tourists will provide Cuban spies unprecedented access to assess and recruit the next generation of American spies. Home field advantage will not only provide a secure environment for espionage, but also drive down the cost for doing business.

Third, unrestricted access to U.S. technology will trigger significant upgrades in Havana's technical capabilities for espionage and repression. No longer will it be encumbered by the expense and time delays prompted by circumventing the U.S. embargo.

The fourth benefit will be the end of travel restrictions on U.S.-based diplomat-spies. This advantage will eventually be further enhanced by the opening of an Embassy, as well as consulates and Prensa Latina offices. I will remind everyone that when the U.S. broke relations with Cuba in 1961, Havana had 28 consulates from coast to coast, and Prensa Latina offices and correspondents in half a dozen cities.

The fifth gain to Cuba is a huge boost in the notion that Cuba poses no threat to the United States. This well-choreographed myth has been aggressively promoted by the regime for the last five decades. The advantage the administration gave Havana with this new initiative elevates this fairy tale to heights Havana could not have achieved on its own.

I would like to conclude by making a single recommendation to the committee. Do everything in your power to degrade or defeat Cuba's intelligence operations. Havana's appetite for U.S. secrets is voracious, and our failure to counter their spying simply fuels their addiction. Expanding relations accomplishes nothing—nothing other than to make Cuban intelligence more effective, efficient, and profitable than it has ever been.

I hope this hearing will help educate all parties as to the high costs of ill-advised outreach. I am grateful for the opportunity to be here today, and I look forward to the question and answer period.

[The prepared statement of Mr. Simmons follows:]

**Hearing before the House Committee on Foreign Affairs**
**Subcommittee on the Western Hemisphere**
**"The President's New Cuba Policy and U.S. National Security"**

**Statement of**
**Christopher Scott Simmons**
**Founder, *Cuba Confidential***
**February 26, 2015**

Mr. Chairman,

Thank you the opportunity to testify on the national security threat posed by Cuba. As Washington considers a radical change in our relationship with Havana, Cuba's world-class espionage operations against us demand careful review and deliberation.

I had the privilege of serving as a Counterintelligence Officer with the US Army and Defense Intelligence Agency for over 20 years. With regard to Cuba, I was deeply involved with most US Counterintelligence successes against Havana from 1996-2004. I was a central figure in the Ana Montes spy case and the lead military official in the 2003 expulsion of 14 Cuban diplomat-spies.

### Cuba as a national security state

Underestimated and misunderstood for more than half a century, Havana remains a clear and present danger to the United States. It is a national security state and its military and intelligence agencies exist solely to ensure regime continuity. Its spy services are augmented by a million-member neighborhood informant program known as the Committees for the Defense of the Revolution (CDRs). These entities combine to give the regime an omnipresent intelligence structure that is – on a per capita basis - 34 times larger than the US Intelligence Community.

Castro's spies also benefit from a narrow focus on just two enemies: the Cuban people and the United States. In fact, the regime has three separate intelligence agencies arrayed against the United States. One of these services, the vaunted Directorate of Intelligence (DI), is ranked 5th or 6th best in the world.

Greed, not self-defense, is Cuba's sole motive for its espionage efforts against the United States. Havana long ago earned the nickname "Intelligence Trafficker to the World" for its sale and barter of stolen US secrets. Following the breakup of the Soviet Union and the loss of Moscow's $3 billion annual subsidy, its auctioning of US classified information skyrocketed. Cuba's intelligence brokering is now reportedly a key revenue stream, earning hundreds of millions of dollars annually in cash, goods, and services for the regime.

## US Counterintelligence vulnerabilities

The administration's current outreach offers five seemingly unanticipated consequences which Havana will exploit as catalysts to increase US targeting.

First, opening Cuba to US travelers will bring a huge influx of desperately needed cash to Cuba's intelligence and security services that – along with their military brethren – run every major component of the tourism industry as profit-making enterprises.

Second, this flood of American tourists will provide Cuban spies unprecedented opportunities to assess and recruit new American traitors. "Home field advantage" will not only provide a secure environment for espionage, but also drive down Havana's costs.

Third, unrestricted access to US technology will trigger significant upgrades in Havana's technical capabilities for espionage and internal repression. No longer will it be encumbered by the expense and time delays prompted by circumventing the US embargo.

The fourth benefit will be the end of travel restrictions on its US-based diplomat-spies. This advantage will eventually be further enhanced by the opening of an Embassy, as well as consulates and *Prensa Latina* (PRELA) offices. As a reminder, when the US broke relations with Cuba in 1961, Havana had 28 Consulates in the US. Concurrently, the PRELA news agency had offices and correspondents in New York, Washington, Chicago, Los Angeles, San Francisco, Miami, Denver, and Atlanta.

The fifth gain is a huge boost in the notion that Cuba poses "no threat" to the US. This well-choreographed myth has been aggressively promoted by the regime for five decades. The advantage the administration gave Havana with his new initiative elevates this fairy tale to heights Havana could not have achieved by itself.

## Recommendations & Conclusion

I would like to conclude by making a single recommendation to the Committee. Do everything in your power to degrade or defeat Cuba's intelligence operations. Havana's appetite for US secrets is voracious and our failure to counter their spying fuels their addiction. Expanding relations accomplishes nothing other than to make Cuban Intelligence more effective, efficient, and profitable than it's ever been.

I hope this hearing will help educate all parties as to the high costs of this ill-advised outreach. I am grateful for the opportunity to be here today and look forward to the forthcoming Q&A period.

Mr. DUNCAN. I thank the gentleman for his comments.

Mr. Menéndez is recognized for 5 minutes.

## STATEMENT OF MR. FERNANDO MENÉNDEZ, SENIOR FELLOW, CENTER FOR A SECURE FREE SOCIETY

Mr. MENÉ NDEZ. Thank you, Mr. Chairman, Ranking Member Sires——

Mr. DUNCAN. Just pull that mic just a little bit closer to your mouth, and it will make it easier. Thanks.

Mr. MENÉNDEZ. All right. Thank you, Mr. Chairman, Ranking Member Sires, and distinguished members of the committee. It is an honor to be here and to be asked to share my analysis with you this morning. I will give a little bit of context in my analysis on three issues—economic changes in Cuba, political changes, and national security implications of Cuban efforts.

Mr. Chairman, of events in Cuba, it can be safely said that the more things change, the more they stay the same. Economically, while Cuba has undertaken a number of reforms, the efforts reflect chronic problems and the inability of the command economy to meet the needs of its population. The urgency of this open secret was made public when Raul Castro declared in 2010 that either we change or we sink.

The reforms, however, are limited, slow, tentative, reflecting internal differences among the ruling circles about their desirability. What remains the same, however, is the military's control, as others have mentioned, of the $3 billion a year tourism industry. This helps explain why inflows of foreign investment, trade, and currency from Canada, the European Union, and countless other numbers—other countries have not resulted in generalized prosperity for the majority.

Politically, in Cuba, there is an existential crisis combining the physical disappearance of the historic leadership and the emergence of a new generation of leaders. While the new leaders are the product of the last 50 years, they lack significant experience in making unsupervised decisions and policy. If, and when, they consolidate their power, the question will remain whether they will follow the current course or begin to respond to the aspirations of a new generation of Cubans who, unlike their parents, are not prepared to sacrifice their lives for a utopia that will never come.

What remains the same is that when Raul Castro responded to U.S. and treaties to normalize relations, he appeared in military uniform, making it unequivocally clear who remains in charge. Through its alliances with Venezuela and the other ALBA countries, Cuba has gained considerable legitimacy by establishing, hosting, and presiding over CELAC, the Community of Latin American and Caribbean States, remarkable by its absence of Canada and the United States.

Meanwhile, Cuban intelligence and security apparatus have projected themselves across the Americas. For instance, through ALBA, they have designed—Cuba has designed the biometric information system of several countries. In our Canada On Guard Report, which is entered into the record, we site an unclassified document from the Canadian Border Security Agency showing that at least 173 cases of Venezuelan passports were issued to Middle

Eastern nationals to circumvent Canada's immigration system. these 173 are merely the ones that we know about. In the current global climate, these types of activities present a clear and present danger to U.S. national security.

Cuba continues, whether through diplomatic or other means, to pursue its objective of shifting the balance of power in the Americas. This is being facilitated because in the Americas, Mr. Chairman, the United States is visible by its absence.

Thank you.

[The prepared statement of Mr. Menéndez follows:]

Fernando Menéndez

Senior Fellow, Center for a Secure Free Society

Committee on Foreign Affairs:

Subcommittee on the Western Hemisphere

February 26, 2015

"The President's New Cuba Policy and U.S. National Security"

Chairman Duncan, ranking member Sires, distinguished committee members, thank you for the opportunity to share my analysis of Cuban events and U.S.-Cuban relations with you in my capacity as an economist and as an observer of Cuba in the hemisphere. It is an honor to be here.

Mr. Chairman, of events in Cuba it can be truly stated that the more things change the more they stay the same. The chronic economic woes, the political control by a ruling elite and the alliances with nefarious and extra-regional actors have underscored, and often overturned, whatever possible economic and political reforms appear from time to time or the best intentions for normal relations.

Today, as the U.S. considers a new policy toward Cuba it is imperative that we separate intentions from realities and neither underestimate nor overestimate Cuba's strength and threats. My testimony will focus on three areas of concern: economic, political and foreign policy/national security.

## I. Economic

Cuba's chronic economic situation is one of decline and a lack of productive output, a persistent low standard of living reflected in the low incomes of the population and the constant shortages of goods and services. After fifty years, many basic necessities are still rationed and everyday life for ordinary Cubans is a constant struggle for survival.

After an economic downturn in 2008, Cuba rated the second lowest growth rate in Latin America. Capital formation declined from 25 percent to 8 percent, the lowest in Latin America in 2011. The country's trade deficit was at $11 billion in 2008. Real wages have declined 72 percent since the 1989 economic crisis, while average salaries are U.S. $18-20 per month (Mesa-Lago, 2013).

In the last few years, the flow of Venezuelan petro-dollars has allowed a respite. According to Carmelo Mesa-Lago, the preeminent scholar on the Cuban economy, the Cuba-Venezuela relationship amounts to an estimated $11 billion, more than Cuba's yearly relationship with the USSR, adjusted for inflation (Mesa-Lago, 2013). Today, however, the collapse of the Venezuelan project signals the writing on the wall, and the status quo is simply no longer tenable. Changes, of varying nature and depth, are the order of the day.

In a remarkable admission, Raúl Castro told the Cuban central leadership in 2010, "either we change or we sink." Implicit to anyone who has studied the Cuban socio-economic system, and despite the verbal contortions used to mask the reality, the statement is incontrovertible: the institutions of central planning and state ownership of the means of production – socialism – have come into irreconcilable contradiction with the economic and social advancement of the people.

As a result of the enduring and untenable conditions, a series of economic reforms are being attempted. These include: distribution of state-owned land to farmers; dismissing one million state workers and the expansion of private jobs in self-employment and cooperatives, among others. The reforms reflect a pervasive and generalized disenchantment with the status quo. While couching the changes as an attempt to create a "sustainable model of socialism," the reforms include a major attraction of foreign investment, a shift in the labor force from the public to an emergent private sector, and the legalization of private initiative to take up the slack in state employment.

The reforms are partial, slow and tentative. Their tentative nature underscores internal divisions among the leadership concerning the reforms. Like previous attempts at liberalizing the economy during hard times, the fear that they will be rescinded abruptly is palpable. The formulations being used to prepare the population for economic reforms and for future inflows of American dollars further mask the central problem of the leadership, that of power, the defense of which may require changes in the economic area. The concentration of power in a ruling group, not any particular social or economic system, is the definition of "the revolution" in Cuba today. This internal dynamic provides a context for the effects of U.S. normalizing relations and the prospect of removing the embargo.

## The Tourist Trap

In the popular mind, as well as among political actors, normalized Cuba-U.S. relations and an end to the embargo are expected to flood Cuba with tourists, dollars, goods and investors.

To assume that dropping the embargo will lead to a flow of dollars that will somehow get into the hands of ordinary Cubans and promote economic prosperity is to ignore the nature, structure and operation of the Cuban economy.

For instance, over the decades Canada has had full diplomatic and commercial relations with Cuba. Nearly a million Canadians travel to Cuba annually. They spend Canadian dollars, trade all manner of goods, and invest in joint ventures. The same is true of the European Union and a host of other countries. Yet, the Cuban standard of living has not improved. In fact, real wages are 28 percent of what they were in 1989.

For one thing, in Cuba the military owns and controls the tourist industry, accounting for some $2-3 billion a year. The armed forces own and operate GAVIOTA, the large tourism conglomerate and it also owns a 51 percent stake in joint ventures with companies like Spain's Sol Melía.

While budget conscious tourists can get a bargain by paying $150 a night for a hotel run in Havana or Varadero Beach, the housekeeper who makes the beds and cleans your room takes home the equivalent of $20 a month. The difference after costs are paid out goes to Gaviota, the armed forces tourism enterprise.

Gaviota is part of the armed forces holding company, known as GAESA (Grupo Administrativo Empresarial, S.A.), or Enterprise Management Group. GAESA is one of the most important entities in earning and controlling foreign currency, and operates a network of import and other goods distribution centers. The chief executive office of GAESA is Col.

Luis Alberto Rodríguez López-Callejo, a member of the Central Committee of the Communist Party of Cuba and, until his recent divorce, the son-in-law of Raúl Castro.

While the new economic reforms will undoubtedly channel some of the inflow of dollars to the emergent private sector, the shear increase in the volume of dollars coming into the economy will compensate for any loses to this sector.

The new reforms attempt to emulate a market economy but only to a certain degree. There is a new market for goods and services in which consumers are the buyers and the new entrepreneurs, such as restaurant owners, taxi drivers and small shops, are the sellers. This has made certain long non-existing goods and services available to larger numbers.

What is missing, however, is a market for productive resources, such as capital, land and labor, in which the entrepreneurs are the buyers using their profits to bid for labor and other factors of production. In Cuba, the state remains the owner of the all capital, land and the labor of the work force.

Foreign investors may put up the capital, but the state retains fifty-one percent control, puts up the land and hires out labor at a fixed price. That way they take up fifty-one percent of the profits, whatever rent is due on the land, and they keep the difference between what they charge for labor and the $20 a month average wage of the Cuban workforce.

It is this system that ensures that the first and largest cut of any inflows of foreign currency will go to the government, and particularly to the military. It is also this system that has been in place as a growing number of countries have done business in Cuba without a corresponding improvement in the ordinary Cuban's standard of living.

The interconnection between tourism, foreign currency and the opaque activities of the military should raise serious concerns, while also serving to explain the lack of economic prosperity for ordinary Cubans.

## II. Political

The Cuban leadership also faces an existential reality: the historical leadership is on the verge of physical disappearance. The infirmities, aging and almost daily passing away of historic figures is like a clock ticking away the last vestiges of the central leadership.

Attending the exit of the historic leaders is the emergence of a new generation of Cuban leaders. The new generation is a product of the revolution. Most who have climbed the ladder in the bureaucracy possesses the two essential qualities necessary to rise through the bureaucracy: loyalty to the system and obedience to authority. One must be irreproachably loyal and committed to the system in all of its phases to be considered for leadership positions. One must be obedient and subservient to those in authority.

The new leaders, however, lack experiencing making policy or executing projects that respond to the aspirations of their generation or their class. Similarly, the true opinions and perspectives of people like First Vice President Miguel Díaz-Canel, Foreign Minister Bruno Rodríguez, and North American affairs director Josefina Vidal, who headed the most recent talks with Roberta Jacobson in Havana, are the subject of conjecture since the system has no public forum to deliberative conversations.

Cuba has a tradition known as the "doble moral" or dual morality. This means that people have become experts at saying one thing in public and another in private among confidants. What is said publicly is what determines one's rise or fall in the hierarchy. This dual morality exists at the top as well as throughout the entire system. Top officials, who are constantly watched, may express widespread criticisms in private but these are only used against them when they fall out of favor.

The fall of Carlos Lage, the virtual prime minister and Felipe Pérez Roque, the former foreign minister, is an example of a long list of new leaders allowed to rise to positions of power and then dispatched for disloyalty. Roberto Robaina and Carlos Aldana are other examples of this dynamic that serve as a warning against initiative or an innovative streak.

As a result, we have little access to what may come from this new generation of Cuban leaders when, and if, they consolidate their power and undertake a new project. One may say that Díaz-Canel is a cipher, showing no imagination, no initiative and little charisma, in short, a cog in the machine. The same could have been said about Mikhail Gorbachev when he first came on the scene. It was Margaret Thatcher who assessed him and found he was someone to negotiate with. In a few short years, after unleashing perestroika and glasnost, the Soviet Union had disappeared.

History seldom repeats itself, especially in such a dramatic fashion, but the lesson here is not to underestimate or to overestimate the strength of an opponent. The key lesson is to recognize that events, ideas and actors are all shifting dramatically. In five years, the Cuba we have known will have changed and in ten years it may well be unrecognizable.

We may either respond tactically to unfolding events, dismiss the battles of ideas and ignore changes in leadership. Or we can craft a new strategy that recognizes internal dynamics, external pressures and systemic failures.

A new strategy has to recognize the demographic changes inside the island, and it must come to accept that the primary catalyst for change is the recognition by people that their most desired aspirations are being hindered by the very ideas and institutions that formed their values, worldviews and desires for over fifty years.

This is exactly the condition in Cuba today. The institutions and ideas formed by the revolution function like a straightjacket on further economic, political and social progress. In watching the new generations of young Cubans, desperately trying to connect both figuratively and literally with the outside world, they no longer see themselves mirrored in the revolutionary project. The practices generated by those institutions and ideas have created a certain muscle memory that keeps them from jettisoning the "revolution" completely, but growing expectations and developing aspirations to form part of the larger global village have long entered into proscribed terrain.

The economic reforms, while limited in scope, for instance, are creating a new generation of self-employed entrepreneurs who no longer depend on the state for their livelihood and as a consequence are less sympathetic to its rules and regulations. The unintended consequences of the initial reforms are yet to unfold, but unfold they will. The revolution has neither the ideological instruments nor the institutional capacity to put the toothpaste back into the tube.

There are minor, but significant openings in the area of alternative ideas. Journals such as "Temas" (Themes), for example, includes studies by Cuban sociologists and others critical of the lack of progress made by Cuban women in gaining full equality, as well as the continuing racial prejudice and discrimination against Black Cubans. Similarly, the Roman Catholic Church publishes "Espacio Laical" (Laic Space) providing a modicum of debate and discussion with a critical tinge. These phenomena, however, have historical precedent and are a form of "managed criticism" to win support from Cuba's intellectuals as well as to project a more liberal façade abroad.

The present leadership is attempting to re-write the social contract by combining a more liberalized economic model with continued control of the state apparatus by a ruling group. But even this centrally controlled plan has unintended consequences.

In the midst of these surfaces changes, the reality of power often reveals itself. During the U.S. president's announcement that he would seek normalization of relations with Cuba, Raúl Castro appeared on television to make his government's parallel announcement. The fact that Castro, who makes a point of wearing tailored suits and ties in his international and some national appearances, was wearing his army general's uniform was lost on no one. The message was clear: this willingness to discuss normalization has been vetted by those who are truly in charge of the island, the military.

### III. Foreign Policy and National Security

Looking at Cuba from the outside there is much to commend in its capacity to achieve its objectives in international affairs and much to raise serious concern.

Venezuela's (Bolivarian Alliance for the Americas) ALBA project, financed through the largess of its oil revenues, broadened the alliance of countries supporting Cuba. Its crowning achievement came with the establishment of the Community of Latin American and Caribbean States (CELAC) remarkable by its exclusion of the United States and Canada. Raúl Castro actually presided over this body for a year term, sending the message that an alternative now exists to the U.S.-dominated Organization of American States (OAS) with its Democratic Charter. Rightly or wrongly, Cuba is less concerned with readmission to the OAS because in its eyes the center of gravity has shifted to CELAC.

On the other hand, the United States has largely ignored the Americas in the last period. Chinese economic penetration, while substantial, is still a fraction of US trade and investment in the region, but the real penetration has been political as anti-American regimes, funded by China, have bought time to wreck their economies and thumb their noses at the U.S. Cuba has been in the forefront of propping up these regimes by exporting teachers, doctors, engineers and intelligence operatives in exchange for foreign currency.

In the past decade, Cuba has also projected its power through the presence and penetration of its security apparatus and intelligence services throughout the ALBA countries. Cubans supervise and train in a number of ministries. Personal security details for presidents and high officials are often Cubans. ALBA Defense, Interior and Foreign Ministries are honeycombed with Cuban "advisers" whose recommendations are often taken as orders.

In one instance, Cuba, having designed the biometric identification systems for the ALBA countries, has raised serious concerns. An unclassified intelligence report from the Canada Border Services Agency (CBSA) revealed that from 2009 - 2011 several Iranian nationals were using Venezuela as a prior embarkation point to circumvent Canadian immigration controls and seek refugee status. According to our research at SFS, at least 173 individuals from the Middle East (namely Iran, Iraq, Syria, Lebanon and Jordan) were issued preferential immigration documentation in Venezuela from 2008 to 2012. These were the number of passports identified by regional intelligence officials, and the total of those issued cannot be accurately fathomed.

In "Canada on Guard: Assessing the immigration security threat of Iran, Venezuela and Cuba" published by the Center for a Secure Free Society, the authors concluded: "Regional intelligence officials estimate that at least 173 individuals from the Middle East were provided passports and national ID cards in Venezuela" (7).

In 2003, the Chávez government launched *Misión Identidad* (Mission Identity) program contracting the Cuban state firm Albert Engineering and Systems, Inc. to overhaul Venezuela's information systems for passports and citizen identifications. The new system, known as SAIME (Servicio Administrativo de Identificación, Migracón y Entranjería), had a critical role:

> *Misión Indentidad's* immigration system facilitates the entry of Cuban agents into Venezuela, embedding themselves into various facets of the Venezuelan social missions and national security apparatus. Aside from Cubans, this group also used SAIME to facilitate the travel of Drug Trafficking Organizations (DTOs), Colombian guerrillas, and Islamist terrorists (6).

The SFS report looks at the links between Venezuela's former Interior Minister Tareck El Aissami and Middle Eastern terrorist organizations such as Hezbollah. The use of government-issued identification and passports to embed potential threats from the Middle East into North America via Latin America should be serious concern to U.S. national security.

The SFS report recommends that policy makers conduct independent investigations of such schemes facilitated by Iran and the ALBA countries, as well enhanced intelligence collection and sharing information with allies in the region.

It is clear that ALBA has served as a bridge to both Cuba and Iran in the penetration of Latin America. Cuba has remained clear in its vision and objective to shift the balance of power in the Americas against the United States. Its alliances have ranged from the former Soviet Union, to guerrilla groups in Latin America and elsewhere, to the forums of the Non-Aligned Movement, to its most recent foreign policy iteration, ALBA. Its real or potential alliances with Iran (which holds observer status in ALBA) and other Middle Eastern state and non-state actors are less about ideological commonality and more about weakening "the empire."

The success of its objectives constitute a combination of Cuban strategic clarity as well as the waning presence of the United States in the Americas for some time now.

The recent intention by the administration to normalize relations provides a considerable degree of legitimacy for the current Cuban government. The new policy, based on an assumption that isolating Cuba has failed to meet its intended objectives, comes at a critical moment in Cuba's internal situation: economic conditions that reflect a deeper crises in the country's social-economic system, a historical transition in the leadership of the regime, and a endeavor to find a new rationale for continuing the current political system.

### U.S. Strategy

In elaborating a strategy for the United States it is imperative to guard against underestimating the strength of the Cuban regime to pursue its agenda, promoting changes that are objectively against our own national interests and to forming alliances with open enemies of this country. Underestimating leads to concessions and appeasement that contradicts our most profoundly held values and principles and lets down our guard to real or perceived threats coming from the hardline ideological and military actors in Havana.

We must be aware, for example, that while Cuban intelligence officers are elbow-deep into the high command of the Venezuelan military, that same military is intimately engaged in the drug trafficking activities of the Colombian FARC. To miss that connection is to underestimate an adversary's strength and capacity to do us harm.

Equally important is guarding against an overestimation of the enemy's strength. The existential crisis, the fundamental contradictions building up between popular aspirations and institutional restraints, and the chronically negative economic conditions all place enormous constraints on the regime's ability to maneuver and achieve its intended aims. It is a fundamental error to focus on the enemy's master plan and to ignore that even the most perfectly planned aims and strategies can often lead to unintended consequences.

In our evolving relations with Cuba, we must remain aware of the general context: that the structures and dominant institutions hamper the generalization of prosperity and the gains from trade; that the country is undergoing an inchoate political and generational transition; and that its foreign policy is at loggerheads with key elements of our vital national security interests.

Change does not always come as we might predict. If economic crises generated political and social change, then such change should have come during the "Special Period," when the collapse of the Soviet Union resulted in an estimated 35-50 percent contraction in the Cuban economy.

Today, the possibility of profound economic, social and political change is contained in the rising aspirations of a new generation of Cubans who, unlike their parents, are unwilling to sacrifice their lives for a utopia that will never come.

References

Domínguez, J. I. (2012). Cuban economic and social development: Policy reforms and challenges in the 21st century (Cambridge, MA: Harvard University Press)

Henderson, V. L., Humire, J. M. and Menéndez, F. D. (2013). Canada on Guard: Assessing the immigration security threat of Iran, Venezuela and Cuba (Washington, D.C.: Center for a Secure Free Society)

Mesa-Lago, C. and Pérez-López, J. (2013). Cuba under Raúl Castro: Assessing the reforms (Lynne Reiner Publishers, Boulder, CO)

Mesa-Lago, C. Raul Castro's economic and social reforms (podcast). Tulane University, Roger Thayer Stone Center for Latin American Studies, March 13, 2013. http://stonecenter.tulane.edu/articles/detail/1299/Carmelo-Mesa-Lago-Raul-Castros-Economic-and-Social-Reforms-in-Cuba

Mr. DUNCAN. I thank the gentleman, and the Chair will recognize Dr. Azel.

## STATEMENT OF JOSÉ AZEL, PH.D., SENIOR RESEARCH ASSOCIATE, INSTITUTE FOR CUBAN AND CUBAN-AMERICAN STUDIES, UNIVERSITY OF MIAMI

Mr. AZEL. Thank you, Chairman Duncan, Ranking Member Mr. Sires, my hometown representative Dr. Ros-Lehtinen. Distinguished members of the committee, I am honored to have this opportunity to share my analysis on the U.S. national security implications of the administration's new Cuba policy, and I commend you on calling this hearing on what is often a misunderstood threat to our national interest.

Last year, when The New York Times editorial board and others intensified their campaign for a unilateral, unconditional change in U.S.-Cuba policy, I published an essay titled "WWCD." That is, What Would Castro Do, if the United States were to unilaterally and unconditionally end economic sanctions?

I argued then that not probing how Castro would respond was an irresponsible omission, since the formulation of U.S. foreign policy is often compared to a chess game in which every prospective move is analyzed with an eye to what the adversary's countermove would be. A foreign policy move always seeks reciprocity.

General Raul Castro has now provided a comprehensive answer to my, "What Would Castro Do?" question. On the 28th of January, speaking in Costa Rica, General Castro set his demands. Before the two nations can reestablish normal economic relations, the United States must: 1) unconditionally eliminate all economic sanctions; 2) return to Cuba the Guantanamo U.S. naval base; 3) stop all the transmissions of Radio and TV Marti; 4) compensate Cuba for the supposed damages caused by the embargo, which Cuba now estimates at $116 billion and counting; and 5) eliminate Cuba from the U.S. State Sponsors of Terrorism list.

The General declared, "If these problems are not resolved, this diplomatic rapprochement would not make any sense, and it would not be ethical or acceptable to ask Cuba for anything in return. Cuba will not negotiate on these internal matters which are absolutely sovereign."

With the General's impossible preconditions now known, advocates of unconditional concessions to the Castro regime will likely double down and begin spinning all sorts of dangerous arguments as to why we should stay the course. We will hear perhaps that, "Well, General Castro was just laying out a starting negotiating position or that, since we have tried economic sanctions for so long, should we not give this new policy some time?"

And much more troubling, we may even begin to hear arguments that Cuba may indeed be entitled to compensation from U.S. taxpayers, or that the naval base in Guantanamo is an unnecessary and expensive relic of the Cold War. Distinguished members, when you hear these arguments, just consider for a moment how Mr. Putin and the Russian navy would love to have a warm water port in the Caribbean of the quality of our Guantanamo naval base.

Consider, also, that if we further remove travel restrictions, thousands of small private vessels from South Florida will begin visiting Cuba on a regular basis and may return with hidden cargo. We can all use our imagination as to the nature of the cargo, whether drugs, contraband goods, or human trafficking. Our over-stretched Coast Guard would not be able to effectively monitor thousands of private vessels traveling regularly between Cuba and South Florida.

Given the long-standing and close links between Cuba and Iran, this ocean travel possibility exposes our border security to new and serious vulnerabilities to terrorism and contraband. Moreover, the President's new measures will enrich primarily the Cuban military and will not impede General Castro's close alliance with Iran, Russia, or Venezuela. It is hard to discern how fortifying a totalitarian government promotes democracy.

The new Cuba policy has legitimized the Cuban regime in the eyes of the world. By sanctioning an oppressive regime that violates human rights with abandon, the President has reversed our long-standing support for democratic governance in Latin America.

The gratuitous normalization with an oppressive military dictatorship sends the wrong message to the continent. Every Latin American would-be dictator now realizes that suppressing civil liberties in their countries is not an impediment to having a good diplomatic and commercial relationship with the United States.

Contrary to the argument of some that the new policy will help improve relations with Latin America, our implicit seal of approval over military dictatorship further weakens American influence and prestige in the region. It encourages anti-American leaders everywhere to take positions inimical to U.S. interests as Cuba has done for decades. One unfortunate visual the new policy has conveyed is that taking American hostages can be very rewarding.

Thank you.

[The prepared statement of Mr. Azel follows:]

**Testimony for the Subcommittee Hearing: "The President's New Cuba Policy and U.S. National Security."**

**Presented before the United States Western Hemisphere Subcommittee of the House Committee on Foreign Affairs – Ed Royce, Committee Chairman, Jeff Duncan, Subcommittee Chairman**

**By José Azel, Ph. D., Senior Research Associate, Institute for Cuban and Cuban-American Studies, University of Miami**

**February 26, 2015**

**What Would Cuba Do?**

Mr. Chairman, Ranking Member, distinguished members of the committee, I am honored to have this opportunity to share my analysis on the U.S. national security implications of the Administration's new Cuba policy, and I commend you on calling this hearing on what is often a misunderstood threat to our national interests.

Last year, when the New York Times editorial board and others intensified their campaign for a unilateral-unconditional change in U.S.-Cuba policy, I published an essay titled: **WWCD**, that is, **What Would Castro Do** if the United States were to unilaterally and unconditionally end economic sanctions?

I argued then that, not probing how Castro would respond was an irresponsible omission since the formulation of U.S. foreign policy is often compared to a chess game in which every prospective move is analyzed with an eye to what the adversary's counter move would be. A foreign policy move always seeks reciprocity.

General Raul Castro has now provided a comprehensive answer to my "**What Would Castro Do**" question.

On the 28th of January 2015, speaking in Costa Rica addressing the III Summit of the Community of Latin American and Caribbean States (CELAC), General Castro set his demands. Before the two nations can re-establish normal relations the United States must:

1. Unconditionally eliminate all economic sanctions.
2. Return to Cuba the Guantanamo U.S. naval base.
3. Stop all the transmissions of Radio-TV Marti.
4. Compensate Cuba for the supposed damages caused by the embargo-which Cuba estimates at 116 billion dollars and growing.
5. Eliminate Cuba from the U.S. "State Sponsors of Terrorism" list.

The General declared that "If these problems aren't resolved, this diplomatic rapprochement wouldn't make any sense." And that "It would not be ethical or acceptable to ask Cuba for anything in return... Cuba will not negotiate on these internal matters which are absolutely sovereign."

With the General's impossible preconditions now known, advocates of unconditional concessions to the Castro regime will likely double down and begin spinning all sorts of dangerous arguments as to why we should stay the new course.

We will hear that: General Castro was just laying out a starting negotiating position or that, since we tried economic sanctions for so long, should we not give this new policy some time?

And more troubling, we may even begin to hear arguments that Cuba may indeed be entitled to compensation from U.S. taxpayers, or that the naval base in Guantanamo is an unnecessary and expensive relic of the Cold War.

Distinguished members, when you hear these arguments, just consider for a moment how Mr. Putin and the Russian navy would love to have a warm-water port in the Caribbean of the quality of our Guantanamo naval base.

Consider also that if we further remove travel restrictions, thousands of small private vessels from South Florida will begin visiting Cuba on a regular basis and may return with hidden cargo. We can all use our imagination as to the nature of the cargo whether drugs, contraband goods, or human trafficking. Our overstretched Coast Guard would not be able to effectively monitor thousands of private vessels traveling regularly between South Florida and Cuba.

Given the long standing and close links between Cuba and Iran, this ocean travel possibility exposes our border security to new and serious vulnerabilities to terrorism and contraband.

Moreover, the President's new measures will enrich primarily the Cuban military, and will not impede General Castro's close alliance with Iran, Russia or Venezuela. It is hard to discern how fortifying a totalitarian government promotes democracy.

The new Cuba policy has legitimized the Cuban military regime in the eyes of the world. By sanctioning an oppressive regime that violates human rights with abandon, the President has reversed our long standing support for democratic governance in Latin America.

Since the 1970's, U.S. policy toward Latin America has emphasized democracy, human rights, and constitutional government. Arguably, U.S. policy in defense of democratic governance has not been uniform throughout the world. But until recently, defending democratic values was our long established policy in Latin America. The gratuitous normalization of relations with an oppressive military dictatorship sends the wrong message to the continent.

Every Latin American would-be dictator now realizes that suppressing civil liberties in their countries is not an impediment to having a good diplomatic and commercial relationship with the United States.

Contrary to the argument of some that the new policy will help improve relations with Latin America, our implicit seal of approval of a military dictatorship further weakens American influence and prestige in the region. It encourages anti-American leaders everywhere to take positions inimical to U.S. interests as Cuba has done for decades. One unfortunate visual the new policy has conveyed is that, taking American hostages can be very rewarding.

Finally, General Castro, in order to secure whatever advantages he may be pursuing, may promise some minor concessions. But before embracing his military dictatorship, we should understand the General has made it clear that Cuba will not change its ways.

---

Mr. DUNCAN. Thank you, Doctor.

And, Ambassador Hays, let me thank you for your service and recognize you for 5 minutes.

### STATEMENT OF THE HONORABLE DENNIS K. HAYS, DIRECTOR, THE EMERGENCE GROUP

Mr. HAYS. Thank you, Mr. Chairman. I would like to thank you and the members of the committee for a chance to appear before you today. With your permission, I would like to submit my written statement and then perhaps summarize the points in it.

One of the key issues that I believe has come up is is that a lot of this was developed through the process of secret negotiations. I have some experience with secret negotiations, and certainly with respect to Cuba I can say that we are very bad at them. And we are bad at them not because we don't have skilled negotiators who have good intentions, but rather that the very dynamic of secret negotiations, particularly those conducted over a length of time, reach the point where the purpose is to reach agreement rather than specifically what is in the agreement. And I think this dynamic is certainly played out.

Secondly, Cuban negotiators tend to be very professional, very knowledgeable. They can even be very charming, but they are also extremely focused. My experience in negotiating with the agents or representatives of the Cuban regime is is they have a great focus. Their concern is what is it that we can give to them, not necessarily what it is that they would give to us or do for us along this way.

In my diplomatic training, I was told always to look at intentions and capabilities. In many countries, it is difficult to determine what intentions are, because there are multiple sources of information and power along the way. That is certainly not the case with Cuba. For over 50 years, there has been a very clear intention, which is to harm the United States in every way that it is possible. This is done both through public statements, including those that my colleagues have mentioned made in the last few days and weeks, and it is also with respect to the—to the actions that have been taken and continue to be taken at this time.

In addition to intentions, you also have to look at capabilities, and here I think there is an interesting point. There is a clear pattern over the years. When the Castro regime has resources, it tends to be more active in advancing its goals to the detriment of us. But when it has fewer resources, it is not able to do this. We are all aware that during the time of the special period in the early '90s when the Russian subsidy stopped, also the Cuban foreign adventurism was reduced considerably, and there also were the first economic reforms that have taken place in Cuba, things like the farmers' markers and the very beginning of some small businesses.

Fidel Castro at that time said he was doing this because he was forced to do it, not because he wanted to. As soon as additional resources began to flow in from other sources, these economic reforms were pulled back and the individuals were denied the opportunity to continue to grow and contribute to their country.

I think an important point here is to look—when you look at our embargo, and what is it embargoes do with totalitarian regimes?

They deny those regimes unearned resources. It is a different dynamic that you get when you have an embargo against a more democratic country where you have a population that feels pressure perhaps and is able to reflect that pressure upward to their political leadership. In a totalitarian society, that does not exist.

The purpose of an embargo is to deny unearned resources to a malevolent regime. And I think that is what our embargo was designed to do, and I think it is what it continues to do.

You know, it is almost amusing to see the statements that have come out in the past few days, particularly with respect to Cuba's place on the list of Sponsors of Terrorism. I saw yesterday there was a report out that it is on to us in order to address this and to remove them from the list of terrorism before we can go further with diplomatic relations.

So we have a situation where we have something that they want, which is to get off the list, and we have something else that they want, which is to have full diplomatic relations with us. So everything is what they want; nothing has been addressed with respect to the issues that we have raised. Members of the panel and yourself, sir, have raised a lot of these, everyone from Joanne Chesimard to the actions that are taking place, the agents that are in Venezuela, and down the line.

And on this, you know, having sort of a focus on Latin America, I follow these things relatively closely. One thing that we have not seen, particularly as this rapprochement has come along, is any indication that our friends and allies in Latin America will step up to the plate and condemn the actions, not just in Cuba but also in Venezuela that are taking place at this time.

I think it is important that we stand fast and strong. Our natural ally in Cuba is the Cuban people, the Cuban dissidents, the ones who are prepared to put their livelihoods and even their lives on the line in order to advance the cause of freedom. Cuba will be a great friend and neighbor to the United States again, but it will not be a good friend and neighbor until the Castro regime is removed, and we give the Cuban people a chance to express their will.

Thank you very much.

[The prepared statement of Mr. Hays follows:]

**HEARING BEFORE THE
COMMITTEE ON FOREIGN AFFAIRS
SUBCOMMITTEE ON THE WESTERN HEMISPHERE
U.S. HOUSE OF REPRESENTATIVES
"The President's New Cuba Policy and U.S. National Security"
February 26, 2015**

**Ambassador Dennis K. Hays (ret.)**

Mr. Chairman, I would like to thank you and the Committee Members for affording me this opportunity to appear before you to discuss the President's New Cuba Policy and U.S. National Security.

Let me begin by saying a word about our history of secret negotiations with the Castro regime - we aren't very good at them.

While there certainly are occasions when it is necessary and appropriate for the United States to hold confidential conversations with other governments, secret negotiations involving major policy shifts should be very rare, and appropriate leaders of Congress should be made aware of them as soon as possible. A secret negotiation, by its very nature, rewards the more intransigent side. And often the more open side ends up more concerned with **reaching** an agreement, rather than what is **in** the agreement.

When dealing with any nation that doesn't share our beliefs and values, it is important to consider both the intent and the capabilities of its leadership.

**Intentions**

It is not difficult to determine the intent of the Cuban leadership. We have a fifty-five year history of unrelenting opposition to our national interests and our core values. Further, from its earliest days the Castro regime has done everything in its power to export its brand of tropical authoritarianism across the hemisphere and beyond, causing untold misery.

But has the Castro regime now abandoned the rhetoric and policies of the past? Has it begun a process of liberalization and democratic reform that merits a response from us? Has Cuba abandoned its support of pariah and terrorist states and organizations? Sadly, there is no evidence of such a spirit of reform taking root.

In the days following the announcement of this latest agreement Raul Castro reaffirmed Cuba would remain communist and he accelerated the pace of arrests of human rights activists – over 100 peaceful human rights defenders were reportedly arrested this past weekend alone. A further forty were arrested just two days ago, on the same day he pinned medals on the five convicted spies returned to Cuba.

Further, General Castro has demanded we unilaterally lift all sanctions, return Guantanamo, pay billions in compensations for the economic hardship his own statist policies have caused and remove Cuba from the list of states sponsoring terrorism.

Meanwhile, Cuba continues to support terrorism and criminality throughout the world. The 240 tons of military hardware intercepted on its way to North Korea in 2013 is, of course, just what we are aware of. The Cuban government supports the growing repression and chaos in Venezuela with thousands of Cuban agents in all areas of the military, security forces, and strategic sectors. A hemispheric project spearheaded by Cuba and funded by Venezuela known as "Twenty-first-century socialism," is an overtly anti-U.S. program predicated on class war that advocates gradually co-opting constitutional mechanisms, usurping the democratic process, dismantling individual liberties, and obliterating U.S. influence and presence in the hemisphere. Their goal is to gradually bring about a radical Marxist-Leninist transformation of society by slowly undermining capitalism, democracy, and "bourgeois" institutions and values from within. But Cuba's ambitions transcend Latin America. In 2011, Italy's respected Corriere della Sera reported that Hezbollah terrorists had established a permanent "bridgehead" in Cuba to provide logistical support for upcoming activities planned in the hemisphere. Last November, the Center for a Secure Free Society reported on a Venezuelan and Cuban program to bring militant Islamists into Canada and the U.S. and to send illicit funds from Latin America to the Middle East. Not surprisingly, Cuba's Ambassador to Lebanon met in Beirut with a leader of Hezbollah late last year and declared the recent agreement to be "a popular victory against colonial hegemony."

Raúl Castro has characterized Cuba's relations with Iran as "excellent", building on the foundation Fidel Castro established years ago when he declared in Tehran that, "Iran and Cuba, in cooperation with each other, can bring America to its knees." Cuba has had a nuclear cooperation agreement with Iran since as far back as 1991. Iran, in turn, has provided hundreds of millions in financing for diverse programs in Cuba including biotechnology cooperation that includes dual use technologies.

## Capabilities

Aside from intent, we must consider capabilities. Here again the Cuban regime has steadfastly followed a clear pattern - when the regime has resources it steps up its anti-democratic actions both at home and abroad. In the early days, this took the form of basing missiles aimed at the US and serving as a proxy for the Soviet Union in Africa and Latin America. When the collapse of the Soviet Union resulted in the loss of funding in the early 90s, the regime scaled back its adventurism. Not coincidentally, this was also a time when some economic reforms were enacted, such as farmers' markets and selected small businesses. As Fidel Castro stated at the time, these were actions they were forced to take. And true to form, as things stabilized, these reforms were stunted and withdrawn. The pattern is unmistakable, when the regime has resources it acts in ways counter to our national interests, when it is denied resources; it must pull back and can do less damage.

As is well known, all economic activity in Cuba runs through and is controlled by the regime; money that flows into Cuba by definition goes to support and strengthen the state apparatus. One of the contributions of Fidel Castro to 20th century totalitarianism is that he understood that if you control the economic life of the individual, you control the political life of that individual – and thus society at large. In a country where there are no rights under the law, where your job, your house, your ration card, and your children's education are dependent on the will of the state, there are few protections available to anyone who wants to be able to read, speak and assemble freely, to form a union, to start a business. This total control is one of the keys to the regime's longevity.

Control of the economy provides resources with which Cuba works to export its brand of authoritarianism. Mr. Chairman, one of the common misunderstandings about our embargo is that it was intended to promote "regime change". Embargoes can be effective in promoting changes in democratic societies, where citizens have a way to express their displeasure to the political leadership. In authoritarian societies, however, there is no mechanism for people to express their will and the elite are isolated from hardship. Neither Fidel nor Raul has missed a meal in the past half century. What an economic embargo does, what it is designed to do, is to deny unearned resources that would be used against that nation's own citizens and neighbors. This is the reason the new agreement is of concern. When we provide, even with the best of intentions, additional money to the regime, absent fundamental reform, absent a change in the intentions of the regime, we are funding activities that run directly counter to our national security interests. Is there anyone who doesn't believe that Cuban agents are promoting the violent crackdown on democratic activists in Venezuela?

## Cuba as a State Sponsor of Terrorism

As damaging as providing rewards with no guarantee of reform is, the nature of the regime is to always seek more - as evidenced by Raul's recent pronouncements. His demand that we remove Cuba from the list of nations that support terrorism, a list Cuba has deservedly been on continuously since 1982, is accompanied by no commitment to reform on his part. The Cubans expect us to take this action in return for a few platitudes, if that. And why wouldn't Raul expect this? This has certainly been our pattern.

It is my hope that Congress will take a substantive role here. Any agreement must protect and advance our interests, not solely Cuba's. A basis for agreement should at a minimum include:

1. The return of scores of felons who have fled U.S. justice, starting with Joanne Chesimard and to include the chief bomb-maker of the Puerto Rican terrorist group that killed Americans in New York and the dozens of Cubans involved in medicare fraud who have stolen millions from US taxpayers;
2. The removal of all intelligence and internal security officers from Venezuela, Nicaragua, and other nations in this hemisphere;
3. The extradition to the U.S. of General Rubén Martínez Puente and MIG pilots Lorenzo Alberto Perez-Pérez and Francisco Pérez-Pérez, indicted by a federal grand jury for the premeditated murder of four civilians flying for the US-based humanitarian organization Brothers to the Rescue;
4. The expulsion from Cuba of unrepentant members of FARC, ETA, Hezbollah and other terrorist organizations;
5. Provision of full information on arms shipments to North Korea and the punishment of those officials responsible for this violation of UN sanctions;
6. Support sanctions against Iran; and
7. Stopping Russian and Chinese intelligence agencies from using facilities such as the Lourdes Signal Intelligence facility.

All of these actions could be immediately undertaken by Cuba and would demonstrate a desire to improve relations with the United States. A failure to act on these matters will demonstrate the regime has no interest in reform and intends to continue to operate as a state that supports terrorism.

**The Future and US Interests**

Mr. Chairman, Cuba is home to a large number of brave and dedicated men and women who, despite unimaginable hardship and great personal risk, continue to speak out in support of the basic human rights we so often take for granted. These men and women are the future of Cuba. It is they who we should continue to stand with, not the supporters of a crumbling dictatorship. Cuba will once again be a great friend and neighbor of the United States and a valuable trading partner. That day will come when the Cuban people again have control over their own destinies. But that day will be sadly delayed if we choose to provide unwarranted recognition and unearned resources to the Castro brothers and their military high command.

Thank you Mr. Chairman and Members of the Committee.

Mr. DUNCAN. I want to thank the gentlemen. Excellent. Apparently, it is obvious that you guys have studied the Cuba issue a lot more than elements within the administration. You bring a very concise message to this committee, and it is much appreciated.

I have a message for Raul Castro in Cuba. You can get off the State Sponsors of Terrorism list if you quit sponsoring terrorism, if you quit providing illicit arms to North Korea outside of the embargo. You could probably have normalized relations with the United States if you allowed more economic freedom, personal freedom, freedom of religion, freedom of speech, for the people of Cuba. Make some reforms. We got nothing out of this deal that benefitted the Cuban people.

I asked Secretary Kerry yesterday, "Is the State Department and the President going to remove Cuba from the list?" He said, "We are reviewing it." Staff talked to their staff. Looks like it may be that June is a target date for that. We are not going to give Guantanamo Bay back, not as long as I have a vote in the United States Congress, and I think my colleagues do as well.

I am fearful that we just won't make the lease payment because it is a leased property, at a very affordable lease rate if you know what the lease is. Whoever negotiated that deal needs to negotiate more on behalf of the United States of America.

This is a strategic base for the United States, but we don't want to give that back to Cuba. They can turn around and give it to the Russians to have a warm water port in the hemisphere. That would be wrong. I want to see more freedom and economic opportunity, economic freedom, more freedom of speech, more involvement in self-governance for the Cuban people. Those are things— those are ideals and the principles that Americans adhere to. That is what we would love to see for the Cuban people.

We see nothing out of the Obama administration for the Cuban people. The economic benefit they may get is maybe some artwork purchased on the street by American tourists, but every other economic transaction benefits the Castro regime. It is a national security issue that is the emphasis of this hearing today.

We have got the Lourdes base, which is an intelligence-gathering base in Cuba, 150 miles off our shore. To your knowledge, Mr. Simmons, has the U.S. ever conducted a comprehensive damage assessment of the Cuban espionage against the United States?

Mr. SIMMONS. To the best of my knowledge, every damage assessment is done on a case-by-case basis. For example, with Ana Montes or Kendall Myers, I am not aware of any comprehensive look back over the last 55 years.

Mr. DUNCAN. Do you agree with my assessment earlier that Americans could be targets of espionage should they travel to Cuba and stay in military-owned intelligence-operated hotels?

Mr. SIMMONS. I disagree with the word "could."

Mr. DUNCAN. Thank you. I take it as they will.

Mr. SIMMONS. Absolutely. As I indicated in my statement, for several years now, essentially 20 years almost, since the end of the Soviet aid, the Castro brothers have allowed the intelligence and military services to run the tourism sector as a profit-making enterprise, one in which they are now allowed to recycle part of the earnings into their own intelligence budgets.

So every tourist that says at the Hotel Nationale or any other entity in Cuba not only pays for the spying against them, but allows repression to increase to levels that were not previously achievable.

Mr. DUNCAN. Thank you. So do you believe that more Americans could possibly be recruited to spy for Cuba as a result of this policy shift? And we had the DIA agent that I mentioned in my opening statement. Do you think more Americans could be recruited?

Mr. SIMMONS. I think opening diplomatic relations with Cuba means open season for espionage operations. It also incentivizes what has already been a cash cow for the Castro regime, drives down the cost of espionage, and gives them access throughout the United States, which they haven't had in—since 1961.

Mr. DUNCAN. You know, there is a lot of outage within the American people and with Members of Congress on both sides of the aisle to Edward Snowden's release of security intelligence to Russia. Who would the Cubans possibly give intelligence that they gathered from Americans to?

Mr. SIMMONS. We know historically they have provided information to Russia, China, North Korea, Haiti, any nation that has something to offer in trade, whether it is cash or quarterly weapons shipments from China.

I think a more recent example, if I may, I recently became aware that Cuba ran a long-term penetration of the National Reconnaissance Office until 2012. I have confirmed this with the Federal Bureau of Investigation. The Director of National Intelligence has taken—failed to answer my queries. What I found out from the Air Force, that this long-term penetration was briefed by Master Sergeant Tessa Fontaine to the Director of National Intelligence, and the case apparently ended shortly before our secret negotiations began.

Given Cuba's total absence of a satellite reconnaissance program, my question to the committee would be: Who were they selling that information to?

Mr. DUNCAN. Right. Yes, thank you. I agree. I want to point to something in the remaining time I have got that Dr. Azel had in his opening statement, that General Castro is making demands on the United States for normalized relations. And you say that—and this is from General Castro, unconditionally eliminate all economic sanctions, return Cuba the Guantanamo Bay naval base, stop all transactions of Radio Free American, Radio-IV Martin, compensate Cuba for supposed damage caused by the embargo, which Cuba estimates at $116 billion, and that number is growing. Who knows what the number will be? And eliminate Cuba from the U.S. State Sponsors of Terrorism list. Those are his demands on the United States.

The demands that the United States made on Cuba—can you answer that question? What demands did the United States make?

Mr. SIMMONS. None that I am aware of, and that is why this unconditional unilateral—is what I really fear we are doing, is not asking anything in return. And, unfortunately, I suspect that we may begin to hear some arguments that, again, you know, maybe the U.S. naval base is not that important or, yeah, maybe Cuba is entitled to some compensation, and the like. And that is really my fear going forward.

Mr. Duncan. Spot on. My time is up. I am going to yield to the ranking member, and I will look forward to the second round of questioning.

Mr. Sires.

Mr. Sires. Thank you. You know, one of my disappointments is being that I always felt that the embargo was a pressure point on Cuba, and that we would take the embargo off when we get some concessions, especially concessions that led to a free economy where people could move ahead, where people could have free elections, where you could have actually freedom of the press.

But, you know, as I looked over the years, Cuba has dealt with its economy with every other country just about, and they have made big investment in Cuba, people like Italy, countries like Italy, Canada. But, you know, the more I read is those countries have pulled out of some of these deals. Can you talk a little bit about that? I know Italy closed its hotels and some of the deals that they made with Cuba. Also, some of the countries invested in trying to find oil. They walked out of Cuba. And, in some cases, the Cuban Government just took over the businesses. Can you talk a little bit about that, Dr. Azel?

Mr. Azel. Yes, certainly. A couple of years ago, I believe I was hosting—speaking at a conference of venture capitalists that had flown to Miami, and they were very interested in looking into Cuba. When I mentioned that just that week the Cuban Government found itself completely short of cash and took over all the bank accounts of foreign companies in Cuba, just took over all the bank accounts. Period. It is amazing what a government like the totalitarian regime can act arbitrarily at any given time and just take over bank accounts in that particular case.

Cuba has a history of not paying its debts. That is one of the reasons why we see Cuba in this kind of a situation. And some of these companies that are having adversity in Cuba are pulling out simply because you have to do business with a totalitarian regime in which the regime will be a majority shareholder, for example.

The Cuban Government, the Cuban military, will have to own 51 percent of the company. Just one of the drawbacks, for example, those companies cannot hire their own employees. They have to request the employees from the Cuban Government. The Cuban Government will then send the employees. Interestingly enough—and this in my mind is a form of slavery—the Cuban Government will pay the employees about 3 percent of what the companies are actually paying the Cuban Government. And the Cuban Government retains 97 percent of the salaries of the employees working in Cuba.

Mr. Sires. So I would think that if any company wanted to invest in Cuba from this country, some of those things have to change.

Mr. Azel. Oh, absolutely. And perhaps most important of all you would have to have an independent judiciary that can adjudicate claims. Cuba, of course, does not have anything near an independent judiciary and will act capriciously and arbitrarily at any given time it chooses.

Mr. Sires. But this is not the first time that Cuba has just arbitrarily taken over bank accounts. I remember when I lived there that one of the things they did was that, and they just gave people X amount of money, but they took everything else that was in the bank for the government. So this is a pretty common practice, but it——

Mr. AZEL. It has, and it was done actually by Fidel Castro. Shortly after the collapse of the Soviet Union, he reversed all the changes he had produced at that time. So, yes, this is their pattern.

Mr. SIRES. I was just wondering, Mr. Simmons, how much influence do you think the Cubans have in Venezuela currently?

Mr. SIMMONS. I believe it is fair to say Cubans are running Venezuela.

Mr. SIRES. How many people do you think—how many Cubans do you think are in Venezuela running Venezuela?

Mr. SIMMONS. The estimates I have seen range in the several thousands.

Mr. SIRES. And, Ambassador, I guess you experienced negotiating with the Cuban Government was, how can I say, very enlightening. Do you think we are prepared to negotiate with the Cuban Government now?

Mr. HAYS. Well, sir, I think it is always an issue is is that you have one side, the Cuban side, which is extremely focused on a certain set of results to come. And that set of results is that they are more than happy to take anything we give them, but they do not give anything back in return. And I can tell you from personal experience that is very frustrating when you are trying to—the whole idea of a negotiation is you reach agreement with somebody by giving a little and getting something back.

In the absence of that, and what I fear, is there often is a case— I think as some of my colleagues mentioned—is that over time you justify, in fact, giving the other side what they want, and you don't ask for something in return.

Mr. SIRES. They were currently negotiating with the European Union, and basically when they got what they wanted they just walked out of the negotiations. There is no negotiation going on now with the European Union, is there?

Mr. HAYS. Not to my knowledge.

Mr. SIRES. But they did walk off the——

Mr. HAYS. This is—I mean, there is not just a pattern, I mean it is an actual process that they go through. And, again, for 50 years I think the United States has been prepared to have some kind of discussion with the Cuban Government, but it has to be on terms of having something where our interests are protected in advance, not just their interests.

Mr. SIRES. This is my concern, that they are going to say, "Look, we are negotiating. We have come to an impasse with the United States. I think there is no more negotiations to be had." This is my concern, that we are going to end up holding the short end of the stick sort of.

Mr. HAYS. Yes, sir. As I mentioned, if the goal is to have an agreement, and it doesn't matter what that agreement is, you can always get there. But if you care about what is in the agreement, you need to be very careful.

Mr. SIRES. Thank you. Thank you.

Mr. DUNCAN. I want to thank the ranking member. I think what he is trying to say is past performance predicts future results.

The Chair will recognize Ms. Ros-Lehtinen.

Ms. ROS-LEHTINEN. Thank you so much, Mr. Chairman, and thank you for your testimony, gentlemen. I am going to ask a series of questions. You won't have enough time to answer, but in the second round we will get around to that.

I am just reading about this interesting Jay Weaver story in the Miami Herald that appeared yesterday, and it talks about this incredible enterprise that the chairman cited about laundering—this case was laundering $238 million in dirty Medicare dollars from Florida into Cuba's banking system and how—and, by the way, this money was funneled as remittances. And, you know, part of the changes that the President has made is allowing remittances to be used through—be sent through a general license, non-family members, complete strangers.

So there is going to be even less scrutiny paid to a lot of this money laundering. And if we are cutting Medicare, you just need to look at South Florida and find out who is responsible for a lot of the money not getting to your parents and your grandparents. And I will ask you to comment on that.

But, Mr. Simmons, thank you so much for your great service to our country, 20 years in the U.S. Army and DIA. And I was wondering if you could elaborate on Ana Belen Montes, because for many folks that is history that they just don't even remember who she was, this high intelligence—high-level intelligence officer who was spying for the Castro regime and is now serving a sentence in our prison. She pled guilty because the evidence was overwhelming.

If you could remind us of who she was, why it was important to catch her, what impact she has had in many of the studies that have been given to Congress about whether the Castro regime poses or does not pose a threat to national security.

And, Dr. Azel, welcome back to our committee. It is wonderful to recognize someone who is one of our professors in my alma mater, the University of Miami. Go 'Canes. And I was wondering if you could put Cuba in a regional context. The administration likes to say that everyone in the region supports their initiative, but they forget to mention that the same countries are so afraid of the Castro regime and its ability to export chaos and unrest in their countries.

And Mr. Sires was talking about that, instead of the administration caring so much about this failed policy and how it will benefit the region, don't you believe that this new initiative is really sending a message to our allies in the region that we no longer rate democracy as high. We no longer care so much about the rule of law, human rights, as highly as we used to, because now we have broken all of that and said, "Everything is fine. Everything is fine in Cuba." And is that message not detrimental to U.S. interest in the region long time?

And, finally, Ambassador Hays, thank you as well for your distinguished career in the Foreign Service. I wanted to ask you about your time in the important post as Coordinator for Cuban Affairs. It is my understanding that you left the position due to some disagreements with the Clinton administration regarding Cuban policy. Can you please describe, if you might, why you left, what objections you had with the Clinton administration on Cuban policy.

And we will start with you, and I know we won't have enough time, but we will have a second round, the chairman says, and then you can elaborate. I don't want to take up a whole lot of time.

Mr. SIMMONS. Thank you. Having spent 6 months debriefing Ana Montes, there is no way in under a month I could accurately assess everything she did. Let me suffice to say that in the 16 years that she spied within the Defense Intelligence Agency—and, actually, to precede that, she was directed into the Defense Intelligence Agency by Havana. She initially worked Central America where she worked against our operations in Central America.

During our secret war in El Salvador, she was pre-briefing every Special Forces team that went down range with the intent of warning Cuba and the FMLN Guerrillas where Americans would be and the exact times. In 1987, she actually visited the headquarters of El Salvador's 4th brigade, which was overrun a month later and a Green Beret sergeant was killed in what was then the largest attack of the war.

And while I am not saying she was the only agent that the Cubans had, we know they had agents on the camp. I think that goes to show the height of Cuba's arrogance when they would send one of their—an agent we believe was ranked in their top 10 to one of our biggest allies, and then overrun their camp 4 weeks later.

She was also tasked by Havana to provide warning on the Panama invasion. We know at the time of her arrest she was to be moved over to the Afghanistan Task Force where she would have compromised operations again. And it was the decision of the leadership to arrest her before she could put any more American lives at risk.

We also know that after her arrest the Russians sent essentially a letter of sympathy to Cuba for the loss of such an important asset.

Ms. ROS-LEHTINEN. And if I could—what connection did she have with Congress? Did she have anything to do with writing reports and briefing Members of Congress about the threat or non-threat that the Castro regime poses?

Mr. SIMMONS. Absolutely. For much of her time within the agency, when she became head of the Cuban Political and Military Affairs, she essentially became the lead Cuba analyst for the entire intelligence community. So not only did she help turn on and turn off U.S. collection against Cuba, in many ways she helped shape U.S. intelligence policy against the island.

Ms. ROS-LEHTINEN. Are her reports still——

Mr. SIMMONS. Posted online——

Ms. ROS-LEHTINEN [continuing]. Posted?

Mr. SIMMONS [continuing]. At the Pentagon? Yes, ma'am.

Ms. ROS-LEHTINEN. Thank you. Thank you, Mr. Chairman. I know I am out.

Mr. DUNCAN. Thank you for your leadership.

I will now go to Mr. Meeks.

Mr. MEEKS. Thank you, Mr. Chairman. Let me first ask—I guess I will ask the Ambassador. Is diplomacy easy or hard?

Mr. HAYS. I am sorry? Say that——

Mr. MEEKS. Diplomacy. You believe in diplomacy, I——

Mr. HAYS. Oh, yes, sir. Very much so.

Mr. MEEKS. And is that easy, or is it hard?

Mr. HAYS. Sometimes a little of each.

Mr. MEEKS. Okay. But it is essential, isn't it? Because what I want to do first of all, let the record be clear—and I want Congress to end the embargo, but the President can't end the embargo, so we are not talking about the embargo here. That only can be done by Congress.

Mr. HAYS. Yes, sir.

Mr. MEEKS. We are talking about diplomacy.

Mr. HAYS. Correct. Yes, sir. Well, I think the key of diplomacy is is you have individuals who then have an understanding of the history, the culture, the political pressures, the desires of the people that you are talking to and negotiating with. So, with that, you have a chance to——

Mr. MEEKS. So should we end diplomatic relationships with China?

Mr. HAYS. No, sir.

Mr. MEEKS. Should we end, even though we are in the middle of this right now, diplomatic relationship with Russia?

Mr. HAYS. No, sir.

Mr. MEEKS. And if all of the information that I am hearing thus far about our national security is because Cuba could give something to Russia, who has the most technology, would you think that—does Russia have more spy technology than Cuba? Does China have more spy technology than Cuba?

Mr. HAYS. Well, in all of these instances, I think the United States has an obligation to protect its own interests and to do so as it is appropriate. And I would never say that we do not have discussions and negotiations with, say, the Cuban Government. What I am saying, though, is that it would be very——

Mr. MEEKS. So what we should have, then, is some form of diplomatic relationships as generally is done through Ambassadors, so that we could try to talk and work things out with countries that we have good relations with and countries that we have bad relations with. We would have diplomatic relations right now if those individuals—talking those through.

In fact, even as we go through all of the negative aspects with Russia and the Ukraine right now we still have a Russian Ambassador in the United States, and we still have an American Ambassador talking to Russians, don't we?

Mr. HAYS. Yes, sir.

Mr. MEEKS. Okay. Now, the Cuban people—let me just ask this, and I will ask Mr. Menéndez, because he hasn't said much, since 1961, to date, has the conditions for the people of Cuba improved?

Mr. MENÉNDEZ. No, they have not.

Mr. MEEKS. They have not. So the conditions of the individuals in Cuba from 1961 until the year of our Lord 2015 is exactly the same.

Mr. MENÉNDEZ. No, it is worse.

Mr. MEEKS. It is worse. What have our policies changed since 1961 until 2015? Has it changed? Has our policy to Cuba changed?

Mr. MENÉNDEZ. Our policy has not changed.

Mr. MEEKS. It has not changed. So, therefore, wouldn't it be logical to say that we have had one policy and nothing has changed, that that policy then was unsuccessful. It did not work to the benefit of the people of Cuba, because their conditions have not changed.

In fact, based upon your testimony, given what our policy has been, et cetera, it has even gotten worse. So does that not also say that if something—and the chairman said past performance shows future results. So our past performance also——

Mr. MENÉNDEZ. May I——

Mr. MEEKS [continuing]. Has shown that—I will give you a chance.

Mr. MENÉNDEZ. Okay.

Mr. MEEKS. But shows that we have done this repeatedly, over and over again, and it hasn't worked in over 50 years. And so then that shows that the results probably will be, if we continue to do the same thing with nothing changing, that the result will be the same. We will—there will be nothing that has changed for the people of Cuba who are living in Cuba.

Let me just go to this, because I don't know whether you have or not, but I know I have visited Cuba several times, the last time about 5, 6 months ago. I have had the opportunity to walk the streets freely and just stop people who didn't know that I would stop them and ask them whether or not they think that the policy of the United States toward Cuba—and they did not ask them in regards to the embargo and diplomacy. The President is only talking about diplomacy because that is the only thing he has jurisdiction over.

I stopped some young people, et cetera, and they told me they don't understand why we still have this policy, that it hasn't worked, and that we should change it. If you talk to the people that are living in Cuba, as I did, you know, just not—just stopping folks, not someone that told me that I had to talk to this individual or that individual.

So as I deducted from my visits and trying to talk to people, same thing I have done in other places, is to ask the people that were living there what did they think about our policy. Many of them, they object to the regime and a number of the things that has taken place there. But they want the policy to change.

Mr. DUNCAN. The gentleman's time has expired.

The Chair will recognize Mr. DeSantis for 5 minutes.

Mr. DESANTIS. Well, thank you, Mr. Chairman. You know, the fact that things haven't ''changed'' for the Cuban people, or have even gotten worse under the embargo, to me that is an indictment on the Castro regime. Why have they not changed? Why is life so miserable for those people in Cuba?

And guess what, Mr. Menéndez? There is a world-wide embargo on Cuba, is that why? So do they trade with all these other countries?

Mr. MENÉNDEZ. They trade with practically every country on the planet.

Mr. DESANTIS. And the money that goes into that country, does that go to the pockets of the Cuban people, or does that go to the military and to the regime?

Mr. MENÉNDEZ. Absolutely not directly to the people.

Mr. DESANTIS. So we have evidence about what happens when you engage with more economic activity with this country. Look, if I thought that this would liberate the Cuban people and we would have a democratic transformation, man, sign me up. But this is going to fortify the regime at a time when it is not only weak, when its patron states are weak, but when we can actually look at how old these Castro brothers are and say, ''Man, we could really leverage this for a democratic transition at one point.'' And so I think it is really troubling.

Let me ask you this, Dr. Azel. Assistant Secretary Jacobson was in front of the full committee recently, and she seemed like it is kind of a fait accompli that the State Sponsors of Terrorism designation is going to be removed. Is there evidence that Cuba is still a state sponsor of terrorism right now?

Mr. AZEL. I think that there is. That is really not my field, but I think we see Cuba constantly trying to penetrate the United States in every conceivable way. Recalling a comment made earlier, at the Institute for Cuban-American Studies, I had the opportunity to interview a defector from the Cuban Government, and he actually was the person responsible for setting cameras in the Nationale Hotel to tape surreptitiously American visitors to the hotel.

So Cuba is deeply engaged in trying to generate intelligence and market that intelligence to places like Iran. And I think that is profoundly troubling.

Mr. DESANTIS. Oh, absolutely. And this could be Mr. Menéndez or Mr. Simmons. The Cuban support for the repression in Venezuela, can you discuss that? And also how there is intelligence that then gets shared through there to other terrorist groups throughout the world.

Mr. MENÉNDEZ. Could I answer?

Mr. DESANTIS. Sure.

Mr. MENÉNDEZ. The Venezuelan situation, clearly there are approximately 50,000 to 60,000 Cubans in Venezuela at different levels. Some are doctors, some are teachers, many intelligence. They run most of the Ministry of the Interior, and they have a considerable amount of—let us say that the recommendations that they make are considered orders in the Venezuelan military.

I just wanted to respond to Mr. Meeks. He said that he was making a logical argument. Actually, the argument you made was a non sequitur. It is a non sequitur because U.S. policy is not responsible for the conditions of the Cuban people. It is the system that the Cuban ruling elite has had for more than 50 years that is responsible for the condition of the Cuban people.

It is that system which trades with practically every country in the world and trades with it in a particular way. There is, for example, the Enterprise Management Group called GAESA. Are you familiar with that, Mr. Meeks? Do you know who the person who runs GAESA is?

Mr. DESANTIS. Well, you can continue addressing him, but it is my time that——

Mr. MENÉNDEZ. I am sorry.

Mr. DESANTIS [continuing]. So if I could continue, because he is not going to be able to answer you because he doesn't control the time. But I would like you to continue to engage that.

So let us just assume that maybe he doesn't know, so can you educate us about it?

Mr. MENÉ NDEZ. There is a gentleman by the name of Luis Alberto Rodriguez Lopez-Callejo, big name. He runs GAESA. He runs the holding company for the military. That gentleman is the son-in-law of Raul Castro. It is a family-owned business, Mr. Meeks.

Mr. DESANTIS. Let me ask you, Dr. Azel, about Gitmo. That has been something—obviously, the United States has had a presence at the naval station down there for quite some time. There is a lot of politics with this administration about the terrorist detainees. But take that aside, just the base as it existed, say, pre-September 11, if that were to be returned to Cuba, how could they use that to harm U.S. security interests in the Western Hemisphere?

Mr. AZEL. I would suspect that the next day that the base is returned to Cuba, Cuba would immediately lease it to either Russia or China. The base, as we know, is an excellent facility, very deep waters outside of Guantanamo where submarines can be hidden and very difficult to locate. Cuba will generate revenue by leasing that facility to the Russian Navy, for example, who would love to have a warm water port in the Caribbean.

Mr. DESANTIS. My time is almost up. I just want to say, Mr. Chairman, thank you for being so diligent on this. You know, the President recently instructed the American people not to get on our high horse about jihadists because of the Crusades that happened 1,000 years ago. And yet here he is trying to establish a relationship with the exact same regime that 50 years ago wanted to nuke the United States, and Khrushchev is the one that had to stop that.

And I yield back.

Mr. DUNCAN. The Chair is trying to be fair. Mr. Castro is recognized for 5 minutes.

Mr. CASTRO. Thank you, Chairman, and thank——

Mr. DUNCAN. Actually, Mr. Castro, Mr. Grayson was on the list first. I didn't see Alan over there. So he is recognized for 5 minutes. My apologies.

Mr. GRAYSON. Thank you. True or false. We have gone from a Cuba policy of all stick and no carrot to a Cuba policy of all carrot and no stick. Mr. Simmons?

Mr. SIMMONS. True.

Mr. GRAYSON. Explain why.

Mr. SIMMONS. I think we need to look no further than who it is we are negotiating with. As the Congresswoman pointed out earlier, for the last 5 years we have been negotiating with Josefina Vidal who—in 2003 I was part of a DIA-State Department-FBI team that threw her out for her espionage activities. And now I predict that if we do open—allow an Ambassador to be posted to this country, she will be the first Cuban Ambassador to the United States.

And when you allow an expelled intelligence officer who has devoted her life to working against the U.S. Congress and the U.S. intelligence community and the U.S. business community, that shapes the tone for everything Cuba intends to do.

During the period that Alan Gross was held in Cuba——

Mr. GRAYSON. Mr. Simmons, I am sorry. I have just 5 minutes. Thank you.

Mr. Menéndez.

Mr. MENÉNDEZ. True, sir.

Mr. GRAYSON. Why?

Mr. MENÉNDEZ. Because we don't seem to have a strategy. We seem to—we are talking about negotiating, but we are not negotiating. It is not clear what our national interests are in this situation. It is not clear what the vital national security issues are in this situation. Unfortunately, I don't think the administration has made it clear why we are even doing this.

Mr. GRAYSON. Good. Doctor?

Mr. AZEL. Well, absolutely, there is no question in my mind. And I outlined in my testimony that Cuba—General Castro has outlined his five demands for relationships. We don't know what our demands are. What exactly is it that we are asking the Cuban Government to do? I cannot find anything of substance.

Mr. GRAYSON. What do you think we should ask the Cuban Government to do? And how should we make that a quid pro quo?

Mr. AZEL. Well, in an ideal world, we should ask the Cuban Government to hold free elections, among other things, to let the Cuban people decide how they want to be governed, obviously to release all political prisoners, freedom of speech, freedom of expression, just the normal human rights that we expect.

Mr. GRAYSON. And what do we use as a quid pro quo for that?

Mr. AZEL. Well, right now, I am afraid we have given up our bargaining chips without getting anything in return. In a situation where they may—emerging Cuba in the future, and I don't see any changes with the Castro brothers in power, but where they may emerge a reformer down the line, we would have had the opportunity to offer lifting economic sanctions, to offering assistance of all kinds, if we were to see a genuine transition to democracy and free market in Cuba.

All we have seen is a succession from General—from Fidel Castro to Raul Castro, and perhaps another succession in the future to Alejandro Castro Espin or somebody else in the Castro family.

Mr. GRAYSON. Ambassador?

Mr. HAYS. Yes, sir. Well, I would say we still have some sticks. Obviously, we have an economic embargo. Cuba is on the terrorist list. And the fact that a lot of importance is being placed on these issues right now I think is evidence that the Cuban Government feels that as a stick and is trying to get it removed.

Again, I would never say that one should never have discussions or negotiations. What I say is that let us go into this in a way that we can advance our interests, and then also the interests of the Cuban people. But definitely we still have some sticks at this time.

Mr. GRAYSON. Is there any indication that the Obama administration is saying something along the lines of "If you do this, we will do that. If you don't do this, we will not do that"? Anything resembling actual negotiating? Ambassador?

Mr. HAYS. I am unaware of anything that is worded in quite that way.

Mr. GRAYSON. Should there be?

Mr. HAYS. I would say yes. Yes, sir.

Mr. GRAYSON. And what would be first on your list?

Mr. AZEL. Well, I think the topic of the day seems to be the terrorist list. And, again, there are a whole set of issues there, everything from Joanne Chesimard to withdrawing the agents in Venezuela to cutting ties with Hezbollah and Iran to, you know, returning Medicare fraud practitioners. And all of those are very specific actions. All of them could be undertaken by the Cuban Government at this time. And all of them would be indication that they are, in fact, interested in having a fruitful discussion with us.

Mr. GRAYSON. All right. My time is up. Thank you.

Mr. DUNCAN. All right. The Chair will now go to Mr. Yoho from Florida.

Mr. YOHO. Thank you, Mr. Chairman. I appreciate the opportunity. Gentlemen, I appreciate you being here on this timely subject.

Let us see. Ambassador Hays, number one, I saw you are a Gator. I appreciate that. You and I were there about the same time, so go Gators.

Mr. HAYS. Very good.

Mr. YOHO. In your statement, you said Raul Castro has characterized Cuba's relation with Iran as excellent, building on the foundation Fidel Castro established years ago when he declared in Tehran that Iran and Cuba, in cooperation with each other, can bring America to its knees.

Mr. HAYS. Yes, sir. That was a statement that got a lot of attention at the time, but I think a lot of people have forgotten that.

Mr. YOHO. Do you feel anything has changed since then?

Mr. HAYS. No, sir. Again, you have to look at intentions and actions, and there is nothing in their public statements or their actions which would lead me to feel that they have come to a different opinion.

Mr. YOHO. Right. And as we grow up, our parents warn us, "Don't hang around with that person because they have bad habits. If you hang around and associate with them, you are going to turn out like them." And we look who they hang around with.

Mr. HAYS. Correct.

Mr. YOHO. Russia, China, Iran, Venezuela. And they are all against the ideologies that we have. And so I think the proof is in the pudding there.

Mr. Simmons, did it help—actually, if you guys can answer this real quickly—did it help and improve the lifestyle of the Cuban people? And I think we all said no, right?

Number two, did it increase their liberties and freedoms in accordance with our beliefs and Western ideologies? That would be a resounding no?

Did it strengthen the anti-Cuban Government—anti-American Cuban Government run by the Castro brothers with the release of the sanctions? Or trying to normalize it.

And I just want to make a comment, with my colleague, Mr. Meeks, saying if something doesn't work for 50 years, you need to change it. There are so many things in here, in America, that we should look at—the War on poverty we have been fighting for 50 years. We put $20 trillion into that, and we are going backwards. So just because it doesn't work doesn't mean you stop doing those. You improve on those.

In your opinion, did President Obama's decree make America safer and more secure, in our hemisphere and as a nation? Mr. Simmons?

Mr. SIMMONS. No, it made us weaker and more——

Mr. YOHO. And I am going to come back to that. Thank you.

Mr. Menéndez?

Mr. MENÉNDEZ. No, it has not.

Mr. YOHO. Dr. Azel?

Mr. AZEL. Absolutely not. It has sent the wrong message to the continent, and every would-be dictator now knows that they don't have to respect human rights.

Mr. HAYS. No, it has not.

Mr. YOHO. All right. So one would have to think, what was the purpose of this? And, I mean, I was shocked to see that we gave up the farm again, like we did with Iran, to have some grand negotiation, and we all know the nuclear negotiation with Iran is a farce. You know, the whole thing was built around preventing Iran to have a nuclear weapon, but it sunsets in 3 to 5 years, some people say 10 years.

The time period really doesn't matter, because it is going to sunset, and Iran will have nuclear weapons. And so you have to think about why would the leader of the world's lone superpower—and I go back to 1996 when Bill Clinton said, ''America can no longer afford to be the world's lone superpower.''

And then I look at the policies over the last 10, 15 years, and I kind of feel that. I mean, with what you guys just said, we are weakening America's security, we are weakening our status in the world. Not that we care about status, but we want security, because that is the number one job of this country.

Do you believe, and this may be a tough question for you to answer, that President Obama's decision, was it out of ignorance, incompetence, or design? And if you don't want to answer that, I understand because I have a thought I want to put in there. Nobody?

Mr. MENÉNDEZ. Well——

Mr. AZEL. I will——

Mr. YOHO. Go ahead, Mr. Azel—Dr. Azel.

Mr. MENÉNDEZ. Absolutely by design, and I think probably prior to the administration. And the reason we are seeing it now is because there are 2 years left.

Mr. YOHO. By design. Dr. Azel?

Mr. AZEL. I would agree with that. It is by design, perhaps looking for a legacy or the like. But it was by design.

Mr. YOHO. A legacy of weakening America.

Mr. AZEL. I suspect that would be the end result of this——

Mr. YOHO. You know what? And there are going to be people that will come after me because of these statements. Whether it is ignorance, incompetence, or design, I really don't care the reason, because none of them are acceptable for America in American citizens. We should do everything we can to make this country stronger. And if we are going to negotiate with people, we should have our—not our standards, but I would think people want the liberties and freedoms that we have, and I think this is a misstep of this administration, and I am appalled.

My time has expired. Thank you.

Mr. DUNCAN. I thank the gentleman.

Mr. Castro is recognized for 5 minutes.

Mr. CASTRO. Thank you. Thank you, Chairman, and thank you to the panelists for sharing your testimony today.

I think you would agree, since the 1960s, we essentially have tried almost everything with Cuba, except for direct military action—the embargo, no diplomatic relations, covert action, sponsored military action with the Bay of Pigs. And so I know there has been a lot of thoughtful debate about the President's decision and what it means and what it portends for the future.

And the way I see it, I see the President positioning the United States for the day when the Castro brothers no longer rule Cuba. Fidel Castro is 88 years old this year. Raul Castro is 83 years old. They have already beaten the actuarial tables and can't imagine that, you know, they are going to beat Mother Nature. I mean, at some point Cuba is going to transition out from under their leadership, and I see this action as the President positioning the United States to be there to work with the new leaders of Cuba when that happens.

Now, this is normalization of diplomatic relations. As everybody has noted, the embargo still exists. There is still, you know, this economic component to it that is still in place, but—and I know that you guys disagree with most of my position, but imagine that we hadn't normalized diplomatic relations and, you know, both those brothers are gone within the next 6 months. Then, what would have happened with the relationship between the United States and Cuba?

And my worry there is that if you are not in position already when that happens, I think you are behind the eight ball, because you have got China, who has been much more active in Latin America, for example. I was with a group of Argentineans last week, an exchange group, and one of them asked me, he said—I said I was on the Foreign Affairs Committee. He said, "Are you not concerned with all of the activity that China is conducting and all the business that China is conducting in Latin America?"

And so how do you see that? Let us say the President had not taken this action and the brothers are gone in 6 months or a year. I mean, how would this have been resolved? What would be—in the rosiest case scenario, you know, how would this have turned out? Anybody. Anybody that wants to address this.

Mr. AZEL. Thank you for your question. Cuba is a military regime with a military structure. What we have seen is a succession. We have not seen anything close to a transition as we saw in Eastern Europe.

If the Castro brothers are gone, that would probably be the opportunity at that moment to advance U.S. national interest. If we have already given up all of our negotiating position a priori, then we are not going to be able to influence that next generation.

Mr. CASTRO. Now, we still have the embargo in place, which is a huge economic, you know——

Mr. AZEL. It is a little bit of a shell, and we are undermining it all the time. So——

Mr. CASTRO. And so, for example, and I take your point, you know, but for example they are getting a lot of their energy from Venezuela, right? I was one of the sponsors of the bill to expedite liquefied natural gas exports to other countries. It would be wonderful if we could become an energy supplier, once the Castros are gone, to Cuba—I think most folks would agree with that—so that they are not in the hands of these—some of these nations that are run by rogue dictators.

But it just—it is hard to me to see a benefit in waiting until suddenly the country goes into chaos, because now for the first time in 60 years or so there is going to be new leadership, and then trying to step in in that moment of tumult. I just think that is incredibly hard. The way it exists now, you have already done one part, which is you are at least talking to each other. You know, now I think—I think realistically what is going to happen is we are not going to lift the embargo until those brothers are gone. I think that is what is going to happen.

Mr. AZEL. Well, I hope so. But it is also—the flip side, it is hard to see how fortifying a totalitarian regime advances democracy. And I don't see how fortifying a regime does that.

Mr. CASTRO. Sure.

Mr. MENÉNDEZ. Thank you for that question, Mr. Castro, which I thought was very thoughtful. It is very nice to see a Democrat in this day and age thinking strategically about the security of the United States.

Mr. CASTRO. There is a few of us here in Congress.

Mr. MENÉNDEZ. I know there are.

Mr. CASTRO. Believe it or not.

Mr. MENÉNDEZ. I know there are. There are those Henry Jackson Democrats.

I think that in my opening statement I mentioned precisely that. There is this new generation of Cuban leaders.

Mr. CASTRO. Sure.

Mr. MENÉNDEZ. What we don't know about them is what they really think, because they have been in positions of executing policy, but the policies always come from above. And the historic leadership is, frankly, dying.

So in some ways, if you thought about it strategically, it would make more sense for us to wait to see if in fact this new leadership has a different approach or if——

Mr. CASTRO. I am running out of time. And I just think that it is tougher when you are not talking to anybody over there, you know? Then, all of a sudden, boom, it is all gone and—anyway.

Thank you, Chairman. I yield back.

Mr. DUNCAN. Okay. The Chair will recognize the gentleman from New Jersey, Mr. Smith, for 5 minutes.

Mr. SMITH. Thank you, Mr. Chairman, for convening this very important hearing. And I apologize for being late—I was the speaker at an autism conference—so I will look forward to reading your testimonies.

Let me just say a couple of points. I remember traveling with Armando Valladares, and anyone who hasn't read his book, I strongly encourage that they do so as well as other books written by those who endured torture and incarceration. His book Against All Hope, I have read it twice. I have been with him. Matter of fact, I was with him at the Human Rights Commission when he single-handedly was able to get the U.N. Commission to deploy people to go to the prisons. They got iron-clad promises that nobody would be retaliated against. Everybody was retaliated against, including those who were in prison.

But here is a man who detailed the unspeakable crimes committed by the regime, by Castro, and a whole line of other people who carried out not just orders, but on their own carried out terrible, barbaric acts against people. I mean, he described so many tortures, it was almost like what happened in the Hanoi Hilton that was commonplace, and still is, against these political and democracy activists.

I, frankly, feel rather than rewarding and enabling a dictatorship, because I do believe that the line of succession—we have seen this—you know, the great hopes that people had falsely about Vietnam—and this seems to be a Vietnam model. I have offered, and it has passed three Congresses in a row, failed in the Senate, never got a vote—the Vietnam Human Rights Act—that we should have insisted that human rights went first, and then all of the other benefits, especially the economic benefits, would follow thereafter. That didn't happen.

Vietnam today is in a race to the bottom with China in terms of incarcerating religious believers and democracy activists and journalists and bloggers. The same thing has happened in Vietnam—I should say in Cuba. This is a lifeline—as The Washington Post so aptly said, a lifeline to this dictatorship.

It is not about the transition somehow matriculating toward democracy. This will almost ensure—hopefully it doesn't but could ensure—that the torturers get the baton when all is said and done. And that is what I am very worried about, the Vietnam model and the China model, and you might want to respond to that.

Frank Calzone is sitting right behind you. Frank Calzone, in 2004, was mugged, was hit by so-called diplomats from Cuba when he was at the Human Rights Commission. And I have been with Frank many times to those Commission meetings. He brought forward some horrific, and very damaging to the regime, information about human trafficking and child sex trafficking.

I wrote the Trafficking Victims Protection Act. It is our landmark law on combatting trafficking. Cuba is a Tier III country, sex tourism, where young children are abused. Who benefits? Fidel Castro and his henchmen from the monies that are brought in from that.

It is amazing to me that those issues are not front and center. Nancy Pelosi makes a trip down to Cuba. Did she go to the prisons? Did she meet with the dissidents who are outside? Apparently not. I have tried to go to the prisons for 20 years, and I can't even get a visa. If you go there, you meet with Fidel, say some nice things and couch your human rights concerns in very, very diplomatic speak. You are invited any day of the week.

So very concerned. I am going to make a reapplication to go there. I want to go to the prisons the way the ICRC and others ought to have been done—been doing for the last 50-plus years. So maybe you might want to speak to the trafficking issue, if you would. How many political prisoners, democracy activists, innocent men and women, has this regime tortured years to date?

Frankly, I believe the Security Council of the United Nations should make a referral for crimes against humanity. We talk about Assad and many others and their butchery. What goes on in those prisons is equally egregious, and I respectfully would ask the administration—all of this talk about—and the political niceties, where the horrific details of torture are swept under the table, somehow we will get to that later, or in some kind of human rights dialogue, like we have with Vietnam.

Those human rights dialogues are almost without any redeeming characters to it, because it—and we do the same thing with China, rather than making it centerpiece with our relationship with those countries as we should with Vietnam.

Let me just—so if you could speak to that if you would, trafficking, human rights, how many prisoners, and whether or not a referral might be—Ambassador Hays.

Mr. HAYS. Yes, sir. I will start off.

Mr. SMITH. Quickly.

Mr. HAYS. You are probably aware there were reported 100 arrests last weekend of democracy activists, another 40 just a couple of days ago. And it is one of these things, if you get into a numbers game, and you have someone who is in prison and you let them go on Monday and then you rearrest them on Tuesday, you could say you have released a prisoner but the fact is is that you are still in prison.

The regime over the years of course has a horrific record. All forms of dissent are put down hard. One of the key things I think that the Castro regime does better than anybody is by controlling all of the economic levers on people's lives they are able to control the political levers on their lives.

If you get out of line, you could lose your job, your house, your children's education, not to mention your freedom. And this all together forms a very strong way to repress any kind of democratic thought.

I would just note, Mr. Castro, that the Castros' mother I believe lived to be 96, so we can't just say that this is something that could go away overnight. What we have to be very careful to do is not to freeze in place a system which will perpetuate these outrageous acts.

Mr. SMITH. Thank you.

Mr. DUNCAN. I am going to allow some lenience. We don't have anyone else on the minority side. We were going to have a second round, so I am going to allow a little more lenience here, because members are leaving. But I want to hear this. Human rights is a huge issue I think for both sides of the aisle.

Mr. AZEL. Well, it certainly is. And although Cuba has changed its methodology, in the early days of the regime there were long prison sentences. They have now pretty much implemented a catch, intimidate, and release type of approach to human rights. So the numbers are sometimes hard to get.

I did want to address briefly Mr. Castro, I think it was. I appreciate your strategic concerns. I would encourage you to see—there is an interview with Alejandro Castro Espin, Raul Castro's son. It is a 30-minute interview, was just done in Greece actually. It gives us a glimpse as to what is in Cuba's future, and it is really troubling to see that.

Congresswoman Ros-Lehtinen had asked me earlier about the impact in Latin America. And it is important to note that since the 1970s our policy toward Latin America has emphasized democracy, human rights, and constitutional government. Arguably, our policy has not been uniform throughout the world. This is true. But until recently defending democratic values was indeed our long-established policy in Latin America.

We have now, I believe, abandoned that by sending a message to Latin American leaders that suppressing civil liberties is no longer primarily a concern of the United States, and I think that will become very dangerous for our national security.

Mr. DUNCAN. Okay. I am going to ask that—we are going into another round of questions. And I am going to ask you if you want to follow back up with a little more information in answering some of the other questions, just in the essence of time, to try to get through this.

So I am going to recognize myself for another round of questions. And if you want to address your answer, Mr. Menéndez, to Mr. Smith briefly, I am fine with that.

But I want to ask all of you, do you think that Cuba has given U.S. intelligence to Iran, North Korea, in addition to any other countries? And I ask every one of you that.

Mr. SIMMONS. Absolutely. And I would also remind the committee that we know for a fact that every major U.S. military operation since the 1983 Grenada invasion, Cuba has warned our enemies in advance with the hope of killing Americans.

Mr. DUNCAN. Mr. Menéndez?

Mr. MENÉ NDEZ. Unequivocally. The enemy of my enemy is my friend.

Mr. DUNCAN. Dr. Azel?

Mr. AZEL. Absolutely. There is a gentleman in South Florida who was Raul Castro's secretary that actually flew to Iraq and gave Saddam Hussein some of our plans for the invasions.

Mr. DUNCAN. Ambassador.

Mr. HAYS. Yes, sir. On a daily basis.

Mr. DUNCAN. Okay. I want to shift things again here, because I am not going to take the whole 5 minutes. But, Ambassador Hays, you made a great point in the end of your testimony, what Cuba could do in actually doing something as we open up these relations.

Return scores of felons who have fled the U.S. justice that are currently residing in Cuba. Remove all intelligence and internal security officers from Venezuela and Nicaragua and other nations in the hemisphere. Extradition to the U.S. of General Ruben Martinez

Puente, mig pilots Lorenzo Alberto Perez-Perez and Francisco Perez-Perez, return those, extradite those to the U.S., so they can face justice.

Expulsion from Cuba of unrepentant members of FARC, ETA, Hezbollah, and other terrorist organizations. Provision of full information of armed shipments to North Korea and possibly other nations, because we don't know—Panama helped us catch that one, but we do know transponders have been cut off if ships traveled into Cuban waters.

Support sanctions against Iran. Stop Russian and Chinese intelligence agencies from using facilities such as the Lourdes to spy on the United States of America. These are things that the Castro regime could do. Great points.

Mr. HAYS. Yes, sir. And Cuban negotiators always will try to keep an argument up on a very high and loose level where there is no actual requirement for them to do anything. What I tried to capture here were some very specific things that could be done if in fact they had an intention to reach out to us in some meaningful way. But I would be very surprised if any of this is on the table at the discussions tomorrow.

Mr. DUNCAN. All right. So I will end and just say there is a lot of brave men and women in Cuba who have—in face of adversity have spoken out against the regime and risked being arrested. And a lot of them have been arrested and in and out of prison, brave men and women that I want to see supported through U.S. policies as we move forward.

So I am going to yield time to Mr. Castro, 5 minutes.

Mr. CASTRO. Sure. Thank you, Chairman.

And, Doctor, I will take a look at that video that you referenced and look through it. I guess for a second imagine that we are 20 years down the road, and almost certainly both Castro brothers are gone, and whatever scores there are to settle between the United States and Cuba have at least—we have gone a long way in doing that.

What role, 20 years from now, do you envision Cuba playing with respect to the United States and with respect to Latin America? I mean, what is their place in the region and, you know, their relationship with the United States?

Mr. AZEL. Well, one of the not-so-well-understood situations is that Cuba instills a lot of fear in the Latin American countries. And we tend to think that maybe it is respect for the Castro regime, but it is mostly fear because Cuba has the ability to influence and mobilize Latin American leftist movements against democratic movement in Latin America. So that is one of the dangers.

Ideally, we would like to see a transition to democracy and free markets, in which case obviously Cuba could be a positive influence. But, unfortunately, as things stand right now, what we have seen so far is just a succession and we may see another succession to another military regime of some sort, but not a genuine transition.

The video I referenced earlier of Alejandro Castro Espin makes it very clear that they have already orchestrated a succession in Cuba, and it is not a succession toward democracy and free markets. It is a succession along the same lines.

Mr. CASTRO. Gentlemen, anyone?

Mr. SIMMONS. I would just like to add that the transitions in national security states have a very problematic history. We have seen that in Russia, we saw that in the former Yugoslavia, but the point is well made. The initial transition has already occurred from Fidel to Raul.

Now, given that 55 years of national security are built into continuing the regime, the government will move forward little changed. The only real difference will probably be a little bit more pragmatic approach, but they will stick with what they have always known. That is their comfort zone.

Mr. CASTRO. Sure. Ambassador?

Mr. HAYS. I tend to be optimistic by nature. If you are looking 20 years out, I see a free and democratic Cuba where the people have the ability to read and speak and assemble as they would like to, travel as they would like to, and they will be a great and strong friend of this nation.

You know, one of the things that always bothered me as I would meet people on the island, or from the island, is that you have—probably we are on our third lost generation now of people who just are waiting for something to change in their life, to have the ability to set up a small business to do the sorts of things that you and I take for granted.

Mr. CASTRO. Sure.

Mr. HAYS. And one of the great tragedies is that time is passing and these people are getting left behind.

Last point on that is, you know, I am a Floridian, a Gator, and I grew up, you know, Ralph and El Martinez, their parents. I used to go over and eat rice and beans at their house, and these sorts of things, so I have lived this.

And one of the things that I am absolutely convinced of is, when the moment comes, and when there is a free and independent Cuba, there will be an outpouring of support and help from not just the Cuban community but the entire American people for them, to help them, because it will be a difficult transition. I mean, we can't—there is another hearing to get into all of the problems that are going to come when you release that pressure and things start popping up. But I am optimistic.

Mr. CASTRO. So what is so remarkable, you know, so, for example, in 2010 I was in China for the World Expo. And, you know, in China you can't use Facebook, for example, but they allow internet access. In Cuba, they have essentially been denied even—a lot of people—internet access. I mean, this is a land that has been—has stood still in time essentially, if you look at the vehicles on the street, for example.

And so I think also, the President's action, part of it is a bet that American culture and notions of democracy will ultimately hasten change. You know, and only history will prove whether that was true or not. But I think that is a sincere hope.

And so I hope you are right, Ambassador, that 20 years from now that is where Cuba is, and they are a good, you know, neighbor of the United States and trading partner with the United States, because it is a country with such incredible beauty and incredible potential.

Mr. DUNCAN. The gentleman's time has expired.

Ms. ROS-LEHTINEN from Florida for 5 minutes.

Ms. ROS-LEHTINEN. Thank you so much, Mr. Chairman, and I wanted to give the panelists an opportunity to answer my long-winded question. Maybe we will ask with—we will start with Ambassador Hays.

Mr. HAYS. Okay. Yes, ma'am. Thank you. You had asked about an earlier experience in my life when I did resign from the position of Coordinator of Cuban Affairs. At that time, I was, among other things, negotiating with the Cuban Government over migration issues and related issues.

There also were, of course, secret negotiations going on at this time, which led to a decision. And, again, this is in the wake of the Rafter Crisis in Guantanamo, and what have you, to where we agreed to the forcible repatriation of Cubans who were trying to flee the dictatorship, that we would take people back in chains, back to Cuba, without due process.

And, furthermore, we committed—we, the United States, committed that we would guarantee that individuals who were returned to Cuba would not be subject to penalty. This was a line that was written into their initial document. Three weeks later, that line had disappeared, and in subsequent documents you do not see the guarantee that the United States made to protect these people.

As the Coordinator of Cuban Affairs, I would have been responsible for enforcing this action, which I did not feel was in the best interest of the United States or certainly not the people trying to flee the horrible situation that they were in. I did resign from my position. I should note I did not resign from the Foreign Service and was subsequently nominated by President Clinton to my Ambassadorship. Warren Christopher, a man who will always be close to my heart, was very supportive at this time.

But if I could very quickly link it back to my earlier comments is that part of this is when you do have secret negotiations, when you don't have outside, if you will, or even different voices that can look at something and say whether it makes sense or not, I think we put ourselves at risk. And that was the case then; I think it is the case now.

Ms. ROS-LEHTINEN. And if I might add, and what has changed since you left for a very principled stand—and I congratulate you for that—is that there has been an uptick in the number of Cubans who have left the worker's paradise, and they have come to my shores right there in my Congressional District. And they are willing to risk the thing they have left, their very lives, to come to this country, even though they have been fed propaganda for more than 50 years that says we are the enemy, and that all these countries, they love you, but the United States is the enemy. But where do they want to come when they have the opportunity? Right here.

And many individuals say that we will still continue with the Cuban Adjustment Act and the Wet Foot, Dry Foot, and it is really—would be hard to say how that would stay in place when we have diplomatic relations. And yet this special status is bestowed only to Cubans who might—will fear persecution were they to be sent back, and how could that be true with all these arrangements that we now have in place.

And what is true is that since these secret negotiations have taken place, and now 19 months or so, 20 months, the number of arrests in Cuba have also skyrocketed. There have been 300 arrests in Cuba in the past month, and obviously the message to the Castro regime is we will look the other way, because that is an inconvenient truth for us. So——

Mr. HAYS. If I could just mention——

Ms. ROS-LEHTINEN. Yes.

Mr. HAYS [continuing]. On that again is we would hope our Latin American allies would also speak out against these arrests, but we—to my knowledge, I have not seen that.

Ms. ROS-LEHTINEN. The silence is deafening. And it is no surprise that Nicolas Maduro, the thug of Venezuela, went to Cuba and then the next day these violent attacks on peaceful protesters broke out, and a 14-year-old Venezuelan teenager was shot in the head as he was attempting to go to school, because now legally the police thugs have been given carte blanche that they can fire on peaceful demonstrators and can mortally wound them.

So that is the reward that they get. He gets his marching orders from Cuba and goes to kill his own people in Venezuela.

Thank you so much, Mr. Chairman, for this hearing. Thank you.

Mr. DUNCAN. Thank you.

Mr. Yoho.

Mr. YOHO. Thank you, again, Mr. Chairman. I find this a very enlightening discussion.

Mr. Menéndez, you stated that there is roughly 40,000 to 50,000 Cubans in Venezuela. Does that include military personnel, i.e. soldiers? Or is that——

Mr. MENÉNDEZ. Absolutely.

Mr. YOHO. All right. So that number is—because I have heard numbers up to 100,000. And when they were having the riots in the streets, I think it was last year, we heard of Cuban soldiers on the street shooting into the crowds. Is that factual?

Mr. MENÉNDEZ. There is I believe a special forces team called Avispas Negras, Black Wasps.

Mr. YOHO. Right.

Mr. MENÉNDEZ. And I believe they were involved in some of it. I don't have any actual data, but I do believe that many people have said this, that they were involved.

Mr. YOHO. All right. And then, the way I understand it is President Maduro is surrounded by Cuban Secret Service. Is that correct? Mr. Simmons——

Mr. MENÉNDEZ. Yes.

Mr. YOHO [continuing]. You are nodding.

Mr. SIMMONS. Yes. Ever since the Chavez regime, the security of the President and key leadership decisions are made in conjunction with Havana.

Mr. YOHO. So I see the Venezuelan state as an extension of the Cuban state that has become stronger in their nature and are working through Venezuela. And we already know of Hezbollah coming through Venezuela, getting the Venezuelan passports, going to Canada. I mean, we know that is factual.

Let us see. What do you think the misdirected foreign policy with Cuba from President Obama says to other countries that we have sanctions with? And Iran, with the nuclear negotiations, Russia dealing with Ukraine, China and the South China Sea and what they are doing in there, how does that affect all of our other relationships with those countries? Just quickly, all four of you, if you can.

Mr. SIMMONS. Well, again, going back to my earlier point about the Cuban penetration of the National Reconnaissance Office, the Cuban leadership takes an intelligence-centric view of the world. And so their takeaway on this penetration was, after their agent having been caught, we immediately entered into secret negotiations, so they see this as a reward. And it is hard for them to separate the two. I would suggest that they won't separate the two.

Mr. YOHO. Well, and then you get somebody like Raul Castro, giving the demands when the sanctions can't—well, we will take the sanctions if you do this and this, and it just—it is ludicrous. Mr. Menéndez?

Mr. MENÉNDEZ. I think the negotiations, in and of themselves, are a victory, whether they get anything or not. I think it is just being able to sit down with the United States and say, ''Look, we are legitimate.'' And that is the message that is being sent throughout Latin America, that——

Mr. YOHO. Well, and then look at Iran. I mean, in that negotiation, they are saying, ''Well, heck, you guys gave up the farm here. We are just going to hold those. We will just be silent.''

Mr. MENÉNDEZ. We are 0 for two.

Mr. YOHO. Dr. Azel?

Mr. AZEL. One terrible message that the new policy has just sent to Latin America, and the rest of the world, is that taking American hostages can be very rewarding as it has been for Cuba.

Mr. YOHO. I agree. Ambassador Hays, I have got another question for you, if you don't mind. You say you see a democratic Cuba in the future. What has to happen for that—in order for that to occur? I mean, what are the dynamics that you see transpiring?

Mr. HAYS. Well, I mean, there are a lot of possibilities. Not all of them are good. There could be chaos in the wake of a collapse of the regime. Again, because Cuba for so long has been at a point where there is basically the Castro brothers, and the two of them are one individual, when they are gone, obviously you are going to have different groups that have different aspirations.

Unfortunately, at the moment, all of them tend to be the senior military command, and I think that is what is most likely to follow from that. But Cuba also has a very rich history of dissent of people who are prepared to stand up and fight for their freedom and their neighbors' freedom. That is who I think we should be supporting. That is who I would put my bets on——

Mr. YOHO. Let me add this to——

Mr. HAYS [continuing]. To do this.

Mr. YOHO. Do you see that happening? All four of you, will that happen if America continues to decline in strength and we have a foreign policy that confuses not just our allies but the people that aren't real friendly to us. Do you see that happening in Cuba?

Mr. HAYS. I think the United States—the United States is the primary force in the world pushing for democracy and human rights. And if we lose that position, I don't think there is anyone that can take our place or would take our place.

Mr. YOHO. Dr. Azel?

Mr. AZEL. I think there is a misunderstanding in our foreign policy that diplomatic engagements and commercial relationships leads inexorably to political reforms. Our engagement with China and with Vietnam for nearly 40 years now has shown that that is demonstrably false.

Mr. YOHO. I am out of time, and I appreciate it, Mr. Chairman. Thank you.

Mr. DUNCAN. Okay. I thank the gentleman from Florida.

And we will go to the last Member of Congress, Mr. Smith, for 5 minutes.

Mr. SMITH. Thank you very, Mr. Chairman.

You know, Ambassador Hays, you may recall I held a series of hearings on the Castro-Clinton accords, and I appreciate the very principled stand you took to express your profound displeasure, especially when the benign treatment when a forcible repatriation was about to occur via a U.S. Coast Guard cutter that—and we know—and I remember asking, how do we know that once that person is returned that they are not beaten to a pulp and tortured and sent to—you know, to prison for a very long time. And there was never a good answer.

So thank you for your leadership on that. That accord between Bill Clinton and Castro is infamous—infamous. We enable dictatorship and people fleeing dictatorship, and we sent them back, in violation of refoulement and every other principle of protecting true refugees. So thank you for your principled stand.

You know, several delegations are likely to make their way, and I don't know if I will ever get a visa. What would be your thoughts—you know, when Ronald Reagan and Shultz went to the Soviet Union—and that was at the—you know, the Cold War was obviously fever pitched, nuclear weapons faced at both nations, really throughout the world, but the Soviet Union and the U.S., and yet we made Soviet Jews and human rights the centerpiece of our policy.

Whenever Shultz and others—Secretary Shultz went there, and I went to the Soviet Union many times, and the East Bloc countries, they always met very publicly with the dissidents. Please, your thoughts on delegations asking to visit the prisoners, one; and those who are dissidents out of prison in a very public way—I mean, we had Artunez testify at my hearing just a few weeks ago. What a courageous man, 17 years in prison, and he talked about the very special brand of racism practiced by the Castro brothers against Afro-Cubans.

Dr. Bicet, who we also had appear via a phone hookup, after spending all of those years in prison, he talked about that very special Afro-Cuban discrimination by the regime, which is in a league of its own in terms of its insidious nature. So if you could speak to that as well.

The lessons learned, Bill Clinton, in May 26, 1994, shelved—ripped up his own Executive Order linking human rights with trade. I can tell you beyond any—I think I have held 49 hearings on human rights abuses in China. They don't have a free internet. It is absolutely controlled by the government. The Great Chinese Firewall is intact and, regrettably, catching dissidents and Falun Gong and everybody else every day of the week. It is like a portal into the individual's home or if they go to a cafe and sign in.

Why didn't we learn the lesson? I mentioned Vietnam before, but China as well. China is one of the most egregious violators of human rights in the entire world. They have—the Laogai is filled to overflowing with political prisoners, labor activists, Falun Gong, religious—Catholic Christian, you name it. They are all suffering if they speak out against the regime, and now they are exporting their brand of dictatorship to Africa, or trying to, and elsewhere around the world.

We know for a fact the Europeans, the Canadians, traded to their heart's content with Cuba. There was no amelioration of the human rights abuses because of that. If anything, they got hard currency to continue on. Again, I thought The Washington Post editorial just the other day about the lifeline that has been extended to the Castro brothers and those who follow the dictatorship was very much on point. So if you could speak to that as well——

Mr. HAYS. Yes.

Mr. SMITH [continuing]. And——

Mr. HAYS. Yes, sir.

Mr. SMITH. Please.

Mr. HAYS. You know, I remember the story that this Russian dissident, Sharansky, tells about when he was in the Gulag, and his jailers came to him and laughed because President Reagan had called the Soviet Union the "evil empire" and they were making fun of this. But the message that Sharansky and the other political prisoners took is that there was someone out there who actually cared about them.

I cannot overstress the importance for someone who is a political prisoner to know that someone is aware of their fate. There is nothing worse than being felt that you have been abandoned and forgotten. So I would certainly encourage every delegation that goes to Cuba to insist on seeing not just the dissidents but also perhaps getting into the prison.

And, very quickly, I am often approached by people, you know, "I am going to Cuba, and I am"—I say, "Look, if you are going to go to Cuba, here is what I would like you to do. I would like you to carry a box of Spanish language books with you. And when you get to Cuba, just pass them out on the street or give them to an independent library along the way, and you will have done some good."

But if you want the true Cuban experience, tell the Customs officer on your arrival that that is what you intend to do. I have yet to have anybody come back and tell me they have successfully done this.

Mr. SMITH. Okay.

Mr. AZEL. So we tend to look at foreign policy through the lenses of our own cultural experience, and we tend to think as Americans that if we can just sit down and talk we can solve all the problems.

We fail to realize that when dealing with totalitarian regimes like China and Cuba, that is not the case.

Mr. MENÉNDEZ. I think what Ambassador Hays just said, I want to just add to it. And I would recommend to you that the entire committee make a serious demand, and that demand is that the International Committee of the Red Cross be allowed into Cuban prisons. And I think that is something that could be done on a bipartisan basis and would seriously, seriously aid those inside the prisons.

Mr. SIMMONS. And I would agree and simply add that any time you are dealing with a police state, when you are silent on human rights, that is all the applause they need.

Mr. DUNCAN. The gentleman's time has expired.

I want to—first off, I want to thank Mr. Castro for filling in for Mr. Sires as the ranking member, and welcome to that chair. I also want to thank Albio Sires for his leadership on the Cuban issue from the minority side. He has been a valuable source of information for me personally, and I hated he had to leave.

I also want to thank T&I Committee for allowing us to use the committee room today, and Chairman Shuster, so that is on the record.

And pursuant to Committee Rule 7, members of the subcommittee are permitted to submit written statements for the record, and we are going to hold that open for 5 business days for any statements, questions, or extraneous materials to be submitted for the record and subject to the length limitation in the rules.

I want to thank the witnesses and the panel today, because you provided some valuable information. It was a great exchange on both sides of the aisle here, and we are going to continue delving into this Cuba policy and what it means to the Cuban people and what it could possibly mean to relations and national security for the United States, which was the focus of our hearing today.

So I want to thank the members for participating. And without any further business, we will stand adjourned.

[Whereupon, at 12:08 p.m., the subcommittee was adjourned.]

# A P P E N D I X

---

MATERIAL SUBMITTED FOR THE RECORD

## SUBCOMMITTEE HEARING NOTICE
## COMMITTEE ON FOREIGN AFFAIRS
U.S. HOUSE OF REPRESENTATIVES
WASHINGTON, DC 20515-6128

### Subcommittee on the Western Hemisphere
### Jeff Duncan (R-SC), Chairman

## TO:    MEMBERS OF THE COMMITTEE ON FOREIGN AFFAIRS

You are respectfully requested to attend an OPEN hearing of the Committee on Foreign Affairs, to be held by the Subcommittee on the Western Hemisphere in Room 2167 of the Rayburn House Office Building (and available live on the Committee website at http://www.ForeignAffairs.house.gov):

**DATE:**          Thursday, February 26, 2015

**TIME:**          10:00 a.m.

**SUBJECT:**       The President's New Cuba Policy and U.S. National Security

**WITNESSES:**     Mr. Chris Simmons
                   Editor
                   Cuba Confidential

                   Mr. Fernando Menéndez
                   Senior Fellow
                   Center for a Secure Free Society

                   José Azel, Ph.D.
                   Senior Research Associate
                   Institute for Cuban and Cuban-American Studies
                   University of Miami

                   The Honorable Dennis K. Hays
                   Director
                   The Emergence Group

### By Direction of the Chairman

# COMMITTEE ON FOREIGN AFFAIRS

MINUTES OF SUBCOMMITTEE ON _____ *Western Hemisphere* _____ HEARING

Day___ *Thursday* ___ Date__ *February 26, 2015* __ Room_____ *2167* _____

Starting Time ___ *10:00 a.m.* __ Ending Time ___ *12:08 p.m.* ___

Recesses _____ (___to ___) (___to ___) (___to ___) (___to ___) (___to ___) (___to ___)

---

**Presiding Member(s)**

*Chairman Jeff Duncan*

---

*Check all of the following that apply:*

Open Session ☑                    Electronically Recorded (taped) ☑
Executive (closed) Session ☐       Stenographic Record ☑
Televised ☑

---

**TITLE OF HEARING:**

*"The President's New Cuba Policy and U.S. National Security"*

---

**SUBCOMMITTEE MEMBERS PRESENT:**

*Reps. Duncan, DeSantis, Ros-Lehtinen, Smith, Yoho, Sires, Meeks, Grayson, Castro*

---

**NON-SUBCOMMITTEE MEMBERS PRESENT:** *(Mark with an * if they are not members of full committee.)*

---

**HEARING WITNESSES: Same as meeting notice attached? Yes ☑ No ☐**
*(If "no", please list below and include title, agency, department, or organization.)*

---

**STATEMENTS FOR THE RECORD:** *(List any statements submitted for the record.)*

*"Cuba Says Fast Track to Restoring Ties Depends on the U.S." - Duncan pg. 2*
*Letter to President Obama from Mayors of Miami, Coral Gables, and Doral - Ros-Lehtinen pg. 16*

---

TIME SCHEDULED TO RECONVENE _____
or
TIME ADJOURNED ___ *12:08 p.m.* ___

Subcommittee Staff Director

MATERIAL SUBMITTED FOR THE RECORD BY THE HONORABLE JEFF DUNCAN, A REPRESENTATIVE IN CONGRESS FROM THE STATE OF SOUTH CAROLINA, AND CHAIRMAN, SUBCOMMITTEE ON THE WESTERN HEMISPHERE

» Print

# Cuba says fast track to restoring ties 'depends on U.S.'

Wed, Feb 25 2015

By Daniel Trotta and Warren Strobel

HAVANA/WASHINGTON (Reuters) - Cuba would agree to restore diplomatic relations with the United States in time for the April Summit of the Americas if Washington quickly and convincingly removes the Caribbean country from a list of state sponsors of terrorism, a senior Cuban official said on Wednesday.

Diplomatic ties were severed in 1961, and negotiators for the two longtime adversaries will meet in Washington on Friday, following up on the first round of talks held in Havana last month.

If the sides move fast enough, they could reopen embassies in each other's capitals in time for the April 10-11 summit in Panama, where U.S. President Barack Obama and Cuban President Raul Castro could meet for the first time since agreeing on Dec. 17 to restore ties and exchange prisoners.

A senior Cuban official put the onus on Washington to first strike Cuba from the terrorism list, which can apply sanctions to banks doing business with the designated countries.

"It depends on what the United States does. It does not depend on Cuba," Gustavo Machin, deputy director of U.S. affairs for the Cuban foreign ministry, told reporters on Wednesday. "It depends on whether we are really taken off the list of terrorist countries."

In Washington, a senior U.S. State Department official said re-establishing diplomatic relations should not be tied to Cuba's place on the terrorist list. If Cuba insists on linking them, it could delay restoring ties, the official suggested.

The official said a State Department review about whether to remove Cuba from the list will be completed "very soon," in weeks at most.

"But we don't think that should be linked to the restoration of diplomatic relations," said the official, briefing reporters on condition of anonymity.

Obama would need to inform Congress of any decision to remove Cuba from the list, a notification that requires 45 days to become official, which is not enough time before the summit.

The American side has said Obama's notification alone should be sufficient because Congress cannot overturn the president under current law.

"I cannot say today, right now, if the act of making the announcement would be a sufficient guarantee," Machin said.

U.S. officials have shown a willingness to expedite the six-month review process and remove Cuba before the summit. Cuba was added in 1982, when it aided guerrilla movements during the Cold War.

The United States is insisting that as part of any accord, its diplomats have freedom to travel around Cuba and meet with a variety of Cubans, including dissidents.

The senior State Department official acknowledged it has been challenging to find a bank willing to handle diplomatic accounts in Washington for Cuba, which remains under a variety of U.S. sanctions.

"Both of us have to come to the table in the spirit of getting to an agreement on these things, and not putting so many obstacles in the way that are not linked directly to how we function as diplomats in each others countries," the official said.

(Editing by David Gregorio)

71

MATERIAL SUBMITTED FOR THE RECORD BY THE HONORABLE ILEANA ROS-LEHTINEN,
A REPRESENTATIVE IN CONGRESS FROM THE STATE OF FLORIDA

# City of Miami, Florida

TOMÁS P. REGALADO
MAYOR

3500 PAN AMERICAN DRIVE
MIAMI, FLORIDA 33133
(305) 250-5300
FAX (305) 854-4001

February 24, 2015

President Barack Obama,
Florida International University

Dear Mr. President:

As mayors of the leading cities in Dade County, we extent our warm welcome to you and our best wishes for a successful visit to South Florida.

There are a number of important issues that are of particular concern to millions of our constituents that might be expected to impact the current bilateral negotiations between the U.S. and Cuba. We would be grateful to have your response on how these issues are being factored into the U.S. position on normalizing relations with Cuba.

Cuban secret police have been deployed in Venezuela to direct the repression of peaceful protesters in that country, including students. An end to the presence of Cuban security forces in Venezuela would seem to be in the U.S. interest, as a way to lessen tensions in the region.

The repatriation of convicted American terrorist Joane Chesimard, enjoying asylum in Cuba after escaping from an American prison for what the Federal Bureau of Investigation terms the brutal assassination of a New Jersey State trooper "at point-blank range," is another issue of concern to our constituents. In that regard, we understand the FBI has placed Ms. Chesimard on its list of ten most-wanted criminals, with a standing offer of a reward of "up to a million dollars for information leading to [her] apprehension..."

Removing Cuba from the State Department's list of countries sponsoring terrorism would seem to run counter to both the Chesimard case and to the federal indictment issued by the Southern District of Florida of two Cuban Air Force pilots and the chief of Cuba's Air Force responsible for the murder of three American citizens and one permanent resident over the Florida Straits, in international airspace. Aside from how this may impact efforts to normalize relations, at a minimum, should not those individuals be placed on an international watch list so that if they travel outside of Cuba they could be brought to justice in America? The three were awarded medals by General Raul Castro, who was then Minister of Cuba's Armed Forces.

www.ingramcontent.com/pod-product-compliance
Lightning Source LLC
Chambersburg PA
CBHW081139290526
45795CB00006B/2294